FOOD, DRINK
AND CELEBRATIONS
of the
Hudson Valley
Dutch

FOOD, DRINK
AND CELEBRATIONS
of the
Hudson Valley Dutch

PETER G. ROSE

Charleston · London

THE
History
PRESS

Published by The History Press
Charleston, SC 29403
www.historypress.net

First published 2009

Front cover: Cornelis Dusart: *The Saint Nicholas Celebration* (detail).
Back cover A Dutch *koekplank* used for molding *speculaas* (spiced cookies) flanks a
dinner prepared from seventeenth-century Dutch recipes. Foreground: whole
wheat bread, coleslaw, cauliflower garnished with hardboiled egg yolks, served
period-style in a bowl with parsley-strewn rim; and a plate of cookies. Back:
green salad, meatballs, stew of various meats and vegetables, Dutch/American
olie-koecken, forerunners to today's doughnuts, and a pear-currant tart.
Photo by Richard Jacobs.

Manufactured in the United States

ISBN 978.1.59629.595.7

Library of Congress Cataloging-in-Publication Data

Rose, Peter G.
Food, drink and celebrations of the Hudson Valley Dutch / Peter G. Rose.
p. cm.
Includes bibliographical references and index.
ISBN 978-1-59629-595-7
1. Food habits--Hudson River Valley (N.Y. and N.J.) 2. Drinking customs-
-Hudson River Valley (N.Y. and N.J.) 3. Festivals--Hudson River Valley
(N.Y. and N.J.) 4. Dutch Americans--Social life and customs. 5. Cookery,
American. 6. Cookery, Dutch. 7. Cookery--Hudson River Valley (N.Y. and
N.J.) 8. Hudson River Valley (N.Y. and N.J.)--Social life and customs. I. Title.
GT2853.H83R67 2009
394.1'2--dc22
2008055296

To my mother: for the past
To Don: for the present
To Peter Pamela: for the future

CONTENTS

FOREWORD

In 1651, an inventory was drawn up of the personal estate of a certain farmer, Jan Jansen Damen, who had deceased on the eighteenth of July of that year on Manhattan. His house had only a few rooms (the description of which, based on a contract with the carpenter in 1641, still exists) and even less furniture. But it had a relatively rich inventory, with lots of linen, lace, clothing, pewter and a silver wine beaker, as well as brass, copper and ceramic kitchenware. The pantry contained, among others, four wooden butter molds, two wooden pint measures for milk and two copper griddles for pancakes. As it turned out, in the rear of his house, he literally brewed his wealth out of beer: on the loft, in the cellar and in the brewery the *schepels* of barley malt, wheat, rye and hop ("just arrived from Holland") abounded. Barrels were still full of beer, including black beer, when he died.

According to his will, which also survived, he desired that his maidservant, Cicilje, would be "emancipated and completely released from her slavery" whenever his surviving wife would sell the farm.

Damen was an early example of a successful entrepreneur. Not only did he farm and brew his beer, but he also owned a share in a ship that sailed the coast of America. In fact, he—and other Europeans who crossed the Atlantic to start a new life in New

Amsterdam or along the Hudson—became relatively well-to-do farmers, not ostentatious, but solid and persevering. Calvinists, yes, but beer drinkers, that certainly too.

There are many ways one can try to trace back the history and adventures of those early settlers, Dutch and others. One can look at the architectural traces, the immaterial aspects of diversity and tolerance, the linguistic legacy or traditional customs. It is to the credit of Peter Rose that she has been focusing for a long time on a specific aspect, the culinary traditions of those Dutch settlers in the Hudson Valley. They left us not only cookies and coleslaw but a whole wealth of recipes that reflect the sturdiness of the seventeenth century. It is but one of the many footprints that eventually helped to form the United States of America, but certainly a most pleasant one.

I am glad that I am allowed here to compliment her impressive research in the subject. The book appears on the eve of four hundred years of Dutch-American ties, which started with the memorable journey of Henry Hudson on his Dutch ship the *Halve Maen* and which led to more than fifty years of Dutch presence on American soil. *Food, Drink and Celebrations of the Hudson Valley Dutch* comes as timely as a well-cooked meal, I should say.

Gajus Scheltema
Consul General of the Kingdom of the Netherlands
New York, December 1, 2008

ACKNOWLEDGEMENTS

H *artelĳk dank* (heartfelt thanks) to Consul General of the Kingdom of the Netherlands Gajus Scheltema for writing the foreword to this book. My sincere thanks to Jean Gehring and Dr. Charles T. Gehring, director of the New Netherland Project, for reading the manuscript. All of us involved in New Netherland studies are deeply grateful for his steadfast, but smiling, leadership and support. Dr. Donna R. Barnes, friend and colleague, is also always ready to answer questions and provide helpful comments. Our working relationship has turned into a fun friendship. A warm thanks to my other readers, Andrea Candee, Allison Chernow, Dr. Charles Danowski, Betty Treyz and particularly to food historian Stephen Schmidt, who interrupted the work on his own book to read parts of mine. Steve and Petrus, his dog, have become much-appreciated comrades-at-the-hearth to both Don and me.

I would also like to acknowledge here, with gratitude, George Heron for the lessons on Seneca food ways and Dr. Christopher Whann for his insightful guidance and most helpful conversations regarding the African cacao trade and cash crops. Richard Jacobs I thank sincerely for many pleasant collaborations over the course of more than twenty years and for the photos used in this book. Jonathan Simcosky of The History Press has been unfailingly kind and patient through the entire process of preparing the manuscript and illustrations. My thanks also go to Nancy Terhune for valuable insights and indexing.

When one works on projects like this over a long period of time, one comes to realize how truly important friends are. Fabulous, feisty female friends such as Andrea Candee, Allison Chernow, Fran Dowling, Alexia Jurschak, Mary Beth (Chip) Kass, Pat Larkin, Susan Simon and especially my first friend in South Salem, Betty Treyz, have helped and supported me over the years through some rather debilitating circumstances. I feel fortunate to have friends in the Netherlands, as well, who were always ready to extend a hand or solve a problem. My oldest friend (in terms of friendship), Ria van Trigt, I have known since I was three, but more recent ones—Johannes van Dam, Marcella de Jong, Alexandra Gaba, Gjalt van der Molen, Marleen Willebrands and particularly Marietje van Winter—were also always willing to help.

It is special when a family member turns into a friend, and I do want to acknowledge here my nephew, Wouter J. van Vloten, who has assisted and aided me in too many ways than are possible to mention, and I am very grateful.

Most of all, I want to express my love and gratitude to my wonderful husband, Don, who makes everything possible. Together we are sustained by and deeply proud of our daughter, Peter Pamela.

Parts of the text have appeared in some form in my own two books on the subject and in the following publications. I gratefully acknowledge permission to use them in this book to the following:

Parts of Chapter 3 will appear in my essay in *Explorers, Fortunes and Love Letters: The Dutch Experience in the New World* (working title), Martha Shattuck, editor, Mount Ida Press, 2009.

The text of Chapter 5 ("Taste of Change") appeared in the 1995 catalog of an exhibit entitled One Man's Trash is Another

Man's Treasure: The Metamorphosis of the European Utensil in the New World (Alexandra van Dongen, et al.) at the Boijmans-van Beuningen Museum, Rotterdam, the Netherlands.

Parts of Chapter 7 appeared in *De Halve Maen*, the journal of the Holland Society of New York, David William Voorhees, editor, vol. LXXIII (Fall 2000).

Parts of Chapter 9 will appear in my essay in *Chocolate*: *History, Culture and Heritage*, Louis E. Grivetti and Howard Yana Shapiro, editors, Wiley, 2009.

Some of the material appeared in various articles in *The Valley Table*, magazine of Hudson Valley farms, food and cuisine, Jerry Novesky, editor.

INTRODUCTION

This book represents my research of the last twenty-five years and includes the texts of talks and articles, as well as the results of new investigations. When I started looking into the influence of the Dutch on the American kitchen, I had no idea that it would lead me so far afield and would go on for so long, nor did I expect such a wide interest.

Since I began in the mid-1980s, I have given hundreds of talks on various aspects of the subject. In 1992, I became a member of the Speakers in the Humanities program of the New York Council for the Humanities, and through that program I have lectured all around New York State. Because the seventeenth-century Dutch Masters portrayed many foodstuffs in their genre paintings and still lifes, I have been able to illustrate Dutch food of the period with their art. As a result, I have spoken at many museums with holdings of such Dutch art all around America.

I have been asked to contribute articles to various encyclopedias such as *The Encyclopedia of New York State* and *The Encyclopedia of Food and Culture*, to magazines such as *Gourmet* and *Saveur* and, locally, to *Hudson Valley Magazine*, as well as to an ongoing column in *The Valley Table*. This is my third book on the subject of the influence of the Dutch on the American kitchen.

The first book, *The Sensible Cook: Dutch Foodways in the Old and the New World*, includes a translation of the main Dutch cookbook of the seventeenth century, *De Verstandige Kock*. The second book, *Matters of Taste: Food and Drink in Seventeenth-Century Dutch Art and Life*, accompanied an exhibit by the same name at the Albany Institute of History and Art in 2002. I wrote it with Dr. Donna R. Barnes, and together we co-curated the exhibit.

New research was needed to round out *Food, Drink and Celebrations of the Hudson Valley Dutch*, and you'll find the results in the pages that follow. The book is divided into ten chapters, beginning with a historical overview that will create a framework for the period. Chapters 2 and 3 explain the Dutch diet and the mainstays of that diet. Chapter 4 describes the food ways of the Iroquois, with whom the Dutch traded, as illustrated by the artifacts found in archaeological excavations. Chapter 5 discusses the handwritten cookbooks handed down through generations of descendants of the early Dutch settlers, and Chapters 6 through 8 explain the customs and celebrations brought here by those settlers. In Chapter 9, my aim is to show the Dutch involvement in world trade, and in the last chapter, you'll find recipes that will make it possible for you to have a "taste of the past." *Eet smakelijk*, or *bon appetit*!

Chapter 1

HISTORICAL OVERVIEW

The beginnings of the colony of New Netherland go back much farther than the traditional date of 1609, when Henry Hudson discovered what is now the Hudson River, and are rooted in the Reformation and the Eighty Years' War with Spain. The story follows chronologically.

In the fourteenth and fifteenth centuries there had been attacks on the teachings of the Catholic Church in England and Bohemia. In the Netherlands, the writings of Desiderius Erasmus (1466/69–1536) about the church's various abuses and practices had a great impact on the thinking of the time. Therefore, when Martin Luther disagreed with the church and in 1520 denounced it, he found a ready audience in the Netherlands. Charles V of Spain, a staunch Catholic, issued orders strictly forbidding the reading of Luther's writings and named an "inquisitor" who would find and put to death Luther's followers. It was the teachings of Jean (John) Calvin, a French Protestant theologian (1509–1564) who had founded a college in Geneva from which students spread his teachings, that had another profound impact. A strong and tough opposition to the Catholic Church was mounted in the Netherlands as Calvinism—the Reformed (Protestant) religion—became more and more popular.

Charles V abdicated in 1555 in favor of his sons, Ferdinand and Philip II, who would govern the Low Lands. Philip II continued his father's stringent, cruel persecution of the Protestants. He grew up in Spain and knew nothing of the lands now in his control. He wanted to force on them a central government without their input and named foreigners to several of the most important posts. His imposition of religious persecution, a centralized government and the placing of foreigners in important positions was the impetus for the Eighty Years' War, which started in 1568. Major battles were fought, with victories for the Dutch side when Den Briel, a strategic city at the mouth of the Rhine, was won; when the Spanish fleet was defeated at the Battle of Zuiderzee; and when the Spanish siege was lifted from the city of Leyden in 1574. A culinary note: the liberators who entered the city brought herring and white bread, and the story goes that cooking pots were found outside the city still containing a stew of root vegetables and meat left by the fleeing Spanish. More than four hundred years later, Dutch people still eat herring and white bread, as well as a stew of carrots, onions, meat and potatoes (a modern addition) on October 3, the anniversary of the liberation.

The decisions made at the Union of Utrecht of 1579, when a mutual defensive bond was forged between the Dutch lands, became the groundwork for the formation of the Dutch Republic as a federal state, encompassing the seven northern provinces of the Netherlands. William, Prince of Orange, often called the *Vader des Vaderlands* (Father of the Fatherland) served as the first *stadhouder* (stadholder) from 1579 to 1584, when he was assassinated. His son Maurits followed in his footsteps and led the rebellious republic from 1584 to 1625.

A major defeat for Spain came in 1588 when its armada of some 130 large ships arrived to conquer England and was defeated in the English Channel by the smaller but faster ships of the English and Dutch. This defeat not only curtailed Spain's maritime might but also made England a more willing Dutch ally and in essence saved Protestantism in Western Europe. (The bond between the Dutch and the English was their Protestantism.

The Church of England was considered Reformed, and English delegates were sent to the Synod of Dordrecht in 1618.)

Trade and fisheries—herring as well as whale—were the source of wealth for the Dutch Republic, particularly for the most powerful province of Holland, where Amsterdam was the major transit market for trade goods. The Dutch traded local goods such as cloth, herring, butter and cheese and products from the Baltic states such as grain, wood, flax, iron, furs and stockfish (dried cod) with southern European countries, where they sold them to purchase salt, wine and semitropical fruits such as oranges and lemons. Trade with Germany was important as well, with dairy products, spices, salt and fish exchanged for wood and wine. The important trade cities other than Amsterdam were Enkhuizen, Hoorn, Rotterdam, Dordrecht, Middelburg and Vlissingen. These cities later would play a role in the West India Company, with representatives on its board of directors.

By the end of the fifteenth century, Portuguese traders had found the route from Lisbon to what is now Indonesia. Lisbon became the transit market for Asian products, particularly spices. Dutch traders in turn would buy those goods and sell them in the rest of Europe. But when Alva, general to Philip II, conquered Portugal, the king curtailed the trade with Dutch ships. This had a large impact, particularly on the salt trade (as discussed in Chapter 9), and forced the Dutch to find their own route to the precious spices. Various attempts were made to find the northerly route, but by 1595 a Dutch ship sailed around the Cape of Good Hope to Bantam and returned in 1597. Many others followed, and in 1602 the Dutch East India Company was founded with rights to exclusive trade with countries east of the Cape of Good Hope.

A truce with Spain was declared in 1609 and lasted twelve years, until 1621. Also in 1609, Henry Hudson was hired by the Dutch East India Company to again search for a northerly route to the Orient. In doing so, he came to the East Coast of North America and traveled from Delaware Bay to and up the Hudson River as far as what is now Albany (see Visscher map).

A 1651 Visscher map shows part of the East Coast of North America; note the "skyline" of New Amsterdam. *From the collection of Joep de Koning. Courtesy Foundation for Historic New Amsterdam.*

By 1614, a fur trading post was established on Castle Island (now the Port of Albany), and some minor trading companies were founded.

At the end of the truce, the Dutch West India Company was established with exclusive trading rights in the Western Hemisphere. As the war resumed, part of its intended purpose was for the company's ships to function as privateers and capture Spanish ships. The highlight of these activities came in 1628 with the seizing of the Spanish silver fleet in the Bay of Matanzas by Piet Hein. Schoolchildren today still sing his praises: "*Piet Hein, Zijn naam is klein, Zijn daden benne groot, Hij heeft gewonnen de Zilveren Vloot*" ("Piet Hein, his name is small, his deeds are large, he conquered the Silver Fleet"—as you can see, in Dutch it rhymes). It was financially an event of great importance to the West India

Company, which nevertheless never attained the success of the East India Company.

By 1624, the first colonists arrived in New Netherland (first so named in a document of 1614) and settled at Fort Orange (Albany), along the Connecticut River and on Burlington Island in the Delaware River. Cornelis May became director of the colony until Willem Verhulst arrived. Verhulst was replaced in 1626 by Peter Minuit, who in that same year purchased the island of Manhattan. In 1629, the Freedoms and Exemptions Act was approved by the West India Company. In order to encourage a larger population of the colony, it allowed for patroonships (a patroon is an estate owner having some manorial rights) to be established. The best known is Rensselaerswijck (now Albany County), a vast piece of land owned by Kiliaen van Rensselaer, an Amsterdam diamond merchant and one of the founding directors of the West India Company. Ten years later, another measure of the West India Company opened up the fur trade to everyone (rather than only company personnel). Company ships traded on the Atlantic rim, including South and Central America and the Caribbean Islands (as described in Chapter 9), and were outfitted with trade goods and foodstuffs at their stops in the new colony.

New Netherland had various directors, but the most famous is Peter Stuyvesant, who became director in 1647 of New Netherland, Curacao, Bonaire, Aruba and other smaller areas in the Caribbean conquered by the Dutch. A year later, a peace treaty was signed in Munster, Westphalia, ending the war with Spain. The treaty stipulated, among other items, that Spain recognized the republic's independence and allowed it to retain conquered areas in the southern Netherlands, as well as those areas owned by the Dutch East and West India Companies.

The period from 1652 to 1654 brought the first Anglo-Dutch War, causing the English in America to be seen as enemies who wanted to usurp New Netherland. In 1653, a defensive wall (present-day Wall Street) was built across Manhattan Island after a threat of invasion from New England. Several wars were fought during the New Netherland period. Director Kieft fought a war with the Native Americans around Manhattan Island; during Stuyvesant's tenure in 1655 the so-called Peach War was fought with natives around Manhattan who had attacked New Amsterdam, Pavonia and Staten Island; and in the same year Stuyvesant recaptured New Sweden in the Delaware Valley after the Dutch fort had been conquered by the Swedes the previous year. A five-year conflict with the Esopus Indians from 1658 to 1663 ended just a year before the English naval force, funded by the Duke of York and Albany, captured New Netherland in a surprise attack during peacetime in 1664.

The colony remained in British hands with the exception of a short interlude in 1673, when the Dutch naval force recaptured it and restored New Netherland as a Dutch colony. Through the conditions set at the peace of Westminster, which ended the third Anglo-Dutch War, the New Netherland colony reverted to England in 1674 and remained British until the American Revolution.

It all may seem so long ago, and yet there is still quite a lot of tangible evidence of the Dutch to be found in the New Netherland area today. In the Brooklyn Museum, you will find the Jan Martense Schenck house and the Nicholas Schenck house—Dutch houses full of period artifacts such as a Dutch silver spoon, Dutch tin-glazed earthenware, cooking utensils, pewter ware and a hearth surrounded by blue and white tiles. (By the way, if Dutch tiles are your interest, the Philadelphia Museum of Art has one of the largest collections in the country.)

In the Hudson Valley, the sight of a Dutch barn reminds us of agricultural activities that started with the Dutch settlers of the area. As Vincent J. Schaefer explains in his book, *Dutch Barns of New York: An Introduction*, a Dutch barn is different from all others because of "its roof profile, identifiable even from a distance, its floor plan, which tended to be square…and the support of its roof by a central core structure." The barns were between thirty-five to fifty feet long and thirty-six to forty feet high, with roof angles of seventy-nine to ninety degrees. The

Mount Gulian Historic Site in Beacon, New York, has such a barn that can be visited. The Verplanck barn, with its unique cantilevered overhang, dates to 1720 and was moved to its site from Hopewell Junction. Historic Hudson Valley's Philipsburg Manor in Sleepy Hollow also has a New World Dutch barn and so does the Mabee Farm in Rotterdam Junction, to mention a few. The Dutch Barn Preservation Society helps to preserve or restore barns in our entire area.

Dutch colonial architecture can be found throughout the valley in towns such as Croton-on-Hudson, Tarrytown, New Paltz, Kingston, Rensselaer, Kinderhook, Albany, Schenectady and many more too numerous to mention. Turn to *Dutch Colonial Homes in America* to find what can still be seen today. *Remembrance of Patria*, the catalog of a 1986 exhibit by the same name at the Albany Institute of History & Art, is also filled with information on Dutch material culture.

Historic house museums, as well as the larger museums such as the Museum of the City of New York and the Metropolitan Museum of Art, have holdings of Dutch and Dutch-American artifacts. Not to forget the New York Historical Society in New York City or the New York State Museum and the Albany Institute of History and Art, both in Albany, New York, which own significant collections as well. Crailo State Historic Site in Rensselaer, New York, however, is the only museum that is exclusively devoted to the Dutch experience in the Hudson Valley. It will close for restorations in November 2008, to reopen in July 2009. It has always been well worth a visit but will be even more so with a new permanent exhibit featuring interactive displays, Dutch genre paintings (high-resolution copies) and archaeological evidence portraying early daily life in the Hudson River Valley.

Chapter 2

THE INFLUENCE OF THE DUTCH ON THE AMERICAN KITCHEN

As was discussed, the history of the New Netherland colony is considered to begin in 1609. In that year, Henry Hudson explored the river that would later bear his name. Through his explorations, the Dutch claim to a vast area between New England and Virginia was established, and by the end of Dutch rule, seven decades later, those persistent Dutch settlers had managed to entrench their culture and ensure its continuing effect on this country.

The twelve thousand or so documents from the period, presently partially translated or in the process of being translated by the New Netherland Project in Albany, New York, are not the only remnants of the Dutch period. There are many more, as discussed in the historical overview—some obvious, some not. As a food writer and food historian, my main interest naturally focused on Dutch food ways and their vestiges in the American kitchen. Every day we eat dishes that can be traced back to those early Dutch settlers, who brought with them well-established and well-documented traditions.

Remaining in Dutch archives, among the many documents that help us understand the foods and meal patterns of the era, is a menu from 1631, considered to be an example of the daily fare of the masses in the Netherlands during the seventeenth century.

A sample of a seventeenth-century Dutch document. *Courtesy New York State Archives.*

It includes such dishes as wheat bread soup, ground beef with currants, salted meats, fish, cabbages, beans, peas, breads and cheeses. Pancakes and porridges were common dishes as well.

Menus and account books from orphanages provide especially helpful insights into the food ways of the common folk. A painting by Jan Victors portrays orphans at mealtime in the Municipal Orphanage in Amsterdam. Indicative of the way things were saved is the fact that it still hangs in the orphanage building, now the Amsterdam Historical Museum. We also still have some three hundred years of orphanage menus, written for each season and with appropriate changes in the dishes according to seasonal availability of ingredients.

In the painting, you see the girls at an evening meal. In the foreground, two of them are filling bowls of porridge, with dark rye bread as the accompaniment. On the left, a girl is filling a pitcher with beer, which was the common drink for every meal. Beer, for which the water is boiled, was safer to drink than water, which was already quite polluted. Cities like Gouda (known for

Jan Victors's *Feeding of the Orphans.* The meals for orphanages were carefully prescribed by their boards of directors. Porridge is served for the evening meal, accompanied by beer to drink and dark rye bread. *Courtesy Amsterdams Historisch Museum, Amsterdam.*

its cheeses) and Delft (now famous through the work of Johannes Vermeer) were particularly known for their beers. (See Chapter 3 for others).

The common meal pattern comprised breakfast, a main meal eaten in the middle or late morning, perhaps an afternoon snack/meal and an evening meal. Breakfast consisted mainly of bread with butter or cheese and a *sop*, a thick souplike mixture of bread and vegetables such as greens, onions or cabbage. Beer was drunk at breakfast; and on the farms, buttermilk was drunk as well. Tea and coffee did not become popular until the end of the seventeenth century. Cornelius Bontekoe wrote his *Tractaet van het excellenste kruyd thee* (*Treatise of the most excellent herb tea*) in 1678, which encouraged people to switch from beer to tea (more on tea in Chapter 9).

The main midday meal seems to be the one for which the orphanage menus were given. It generally consisted of no more than two or three dishes. The first one was often a *hutspot*, a one-pot dish of vegetables and some meat, or perhaps a grain-based *sop*; the second dish might be fish of one sort or another, or a meat stewed with prunes and currants; the third dish might be fruit, as well as cooked vegetables. On the farm this meal often consisted simply of a porridge, bread and meat.

While I called this the midday meal, the Netherlands' beloved poet Jacob Cats, so beloved that he was often called "Father Cats," wrote a poem regarding "the healthful life" that admonished readers to rise at six and have the main meal about ten in the morning. Six o'clock in the evening would be the time for another meal, and by 10:00 p.m. it would be bedtime, as quoted in the retranslation into modern Dutch of *De Verstandige Kock* (*The Sensible Cook*) by Dutch food historian Marleen Willebrands.

A few hours after the midday meal, between two and three o'clock, some bread with butter or cheese was eaten by those who needed additional sustenance. Just before going to bed, the final nourishment of the day was served. It could again consist of bread, butter or cheese, but leftovers from midday might be

A *poffertjespan*, made of cast iron, is the modern-day equivalent of the brass pans of the seventeenth-century. *Photo by Richard Jacobs.*

served as well; or a porridge made from wheat flour and sweet milk, or bread and milk, might be offered.

The mainstay of the Dutch diet was bread. (The Dutch still eat two bread meals a day.) The bakers prepared not only regular bread, but also the sweet breads, pastries and *koekjes* (cookies), of which the Dutch were and are so fond. (You'll read in Chapter 4 that in the New World they even used their baking skills in trading with the Native Americans.)

While bakers were responsible for baking the daily bread, made at home were (and still are) waffles; wafers; pancakes; *poffertjes*, which are tiny puffed pancakes the size of a silver dollar, prepared in a special pan with small indentations; and *olie-koecken*, deep-fried balls of soft dough with or without chopped fruit. Waffles were a food for festive occasions. We see them mentioned as part of holidays such as Twelfth Night, Easter and Pinkster or Pentecost.

Pancakes were made at home and served as a meal, but not for breakfast the way we commonly use them now in this country.

Since there are many seventeenth-century paintings of pancake bakers, it clearly was a favorite food. For instance, in a painting by a follower of Nicolaes Maes, we see a woman resting her pan on a tall trivet standing over a lively fire in the hearth. Her batter pot stands by her side. A little boy is holding up his pancake because his dog is trying to get a bite from it. The pancake is not soft and floppy the way ours are, but rather stiff. Dutch pancakes were made with yeast (rather than baking powder) and were quite sturdy, so they could be eaten out of one's hand. In that painting, a barrel is used as a table; on it stands a big piece of golden butter to spread on the pancake.

While orphanage menus and account books tell us about the diet of the working class and the poor, a period cookbook entitled *De Verstandige Kock* helps us understand the food ways of the more affluent middle class. I have translated this book into English with the title *The Sensible Cook*. Written by an anonymous author and first published in 1667 by Marcus Doornick of Amsterdam, it is generally accepted to be the main cookbook of the seventeenth century in the Netherlands. Called "the most influential cookbook in the 17th and 18th century," it had at least fifteen reprints in various forms as late as 1802.

The cookbook is part of a larger volume entitled *Het Vermakelijk Landtleven* (*The Pleasurable Country Life*), which contains extensive sections on orchards, beekeeping, herbs, distilling, medicines and food preservation. In my research on Dutch food ways, I came across this book in the library of Historic Hudson Valley, and other volumes are held in libraries all across America. Since the book contains such a wealth of information on subjects important to everyday life, it seems highly probable that this volume was among the many books that Dutch settlers regularly ordered from the Netherlands.

The Sensible Cook, though printed in the second half of the century, helps us to understand the well-established seventeenth-century Dutch food ways in the Netherlands (after all, cookbooks have traditionally codified already existing recipes). It also helps to create a framework for information

DE

VERSTANDIGE KOCK,

Of Sorghvuldige Huyshoudſter:

BESCHRYVENDE

Hoe men op de beſte en bequaemſte manier alderhande Spijſen
ſal koocken/ ſtoven/ braden/ backen/ en bereyden; met de Sauſſen daer toe
dienende: Seer dienſtigh/ en profijtelijck in alle Huyshoudingen.

Oock om veelderley ſlagh van TAERTEN en PASTEYEN toe te ſtellen

Vermeerdert, met de

. HOLLANDTSE SLACHT-TYDT.

Hier is noch achter opgevoeght/ de

VERSTANDIGE CONFITUURMAKER,

Onderwijſende/ hoe men van veelderhande Vruchten/ Wortelen/ Bloemen en Bla-
den/ etc. goede/ en nutte Confituren ſal konnen toemaken/ en bewaren,

t'Amſterdam, Bp GYSBERT de GROOT, Boeckverkooper tuſſchen de
twee Haerlemmer-ſlupſen in de groote Bybel. Met Privilegie.

Title page of *De Verstandige Kock* in the 1683 edition of *Het Vermakelijk Landtleven*. This was the definitive Dutch cookbook of the seventeenth century. The title page shows the kitchen of a well-to-do household, with two cooks hard at work. In the left-hand corner is a brick stove for which building instructions are given in the book. This kind of stove (forerunner of a modern stove) made it easier to regulate the heat required for the slow cooking methods in many recipes. *Courtesy Historic Hudson Valley, Tarrytown, New York.*

about New Netherland—derived from a variety of sources and archaeological evidence.

The book's recipes abound with what were then rather exotic items of the times, such as lemons, mace, nutmeg and pepper. Spices and wines were among the items that were imported from faraway lands by Dutch seafarers. In the dishes, mace was used more frequently as a seasoning than nutmeg, perhaps because one needs a grater for the nut, but also called for are cinnamon, ginger and other spices we use today.

The Sensible Cook gives the full spectrum of recipes for salads and vegetables—together about twenty-five varieties, including artichokes, asparagus, beets, endive, Brussels sprouts and various cabbages; carrots, celery, chicory, cucumber, fava beans and many varieties of lettuces; leeks, onions, parsnips, peas and sugar peas, pole or green beans, purslane, radishes, spinach, turnips and also a New World import: Jerusalem artichokes. Recipes for meats include the preparation of beef, lamb, mutton and pork, as well as suckling pig, haunches of sheep, veal and particularly several recipes for meatballs, then and now a favorite dish. (In Chapter 10, you'll find such a meatball recipe.) The poultry recipes discuss many ways of making chicken, but also pigeons, ducks, capon, partridges and goose, and they include again a New World import: turkeys. Both Jerusalem artichokes and turkeys reached Europe through earlier explorations of the Americas. For a seafaring nation, it is logical to have a lot of fish on the menu—mentioned in the book are sturgeon, bream, pike, carp, salmon, codfish, tench, roach, haddock, eel, lobster, crab, oysters and mussels, representing both saltwater and freshwater fish. Other recipes are for baked goods, including savory raised pies and pastries such as various kinds of apple *taert*, a baked good made of short-crust dough. A wedge of *appeltaart* (in modern Dutch spelling) is still a very common treat in the Netherlands today.

With its separate section on preserving, the book confirms that food preservation was part of the affluent kitchen. A separate section entitled *The Sensible Confectioner* gives recipes for preserving fruits, including green walnuts in sugar; tells how to make a "marmalade" from quinces; and also contains a delicious recipe for quince paste, which is cut into squares and dried. Since quinces are a fall fruit, these make an excellent addition to today's holiday cookie tray. Fruits are also made into juices and sauces, or dried to be preserved "for a whole year," as the book says.

Another separate section, *The Dutch Butchering Time*, instructs "how one shall supply oneself with a stock of Meat against the Winter." It gives directions on how to prepare a tub for salting meat to preserve it for the cold months and talks about smoking meats and making sausages, head-meat or rolled tripe.

"Cooks in a hurry" seems to have been as timely a topic then as it is today; the book begins with a one-page cooking index in which are mentioned "all dishes that are usually prepared so that if one is in a hurry, this list will help to think of what to prepare." But some of its recipes give the modern cook a chuckle, as in "How to do a good job in cooking young chickens, turkeys, and ducks." Imagine today's hurried cook being advised on "How to prepare live pigeons in one hour and a half." In short, the book gives a full overview of what a well-to-do household should know about food preparation. The book was written for the ever-growing middle class of people who had invested well and could afford to buy country houses with large gardens, filled with fruits and vegetables, for which it gives an ample number of recipes. Because of the amount of vegetables described, it stepped away from medieval cooking manuals and can be seen as a more modern cookbook.

However, it still followed the medical theories of Galen (*Galenus*) of Pergamon of the second century (AD). Professor Johanna Maria van Winter, a medievalist, explained in her book, *Spices and Comfits*, how these theories contain a scheme of

> the four humours or fluids (blood, yellow bile, black bile, and phlegm), that corresponded to the four human temperaments (sanguine, choleric, melancholic, and phlegmatic). Each

fluid belonged to a distinct season and a distinct period of life and had two qualities: blood was humid and warm and belonged to spring and youth; yellow bile was warm and dry like summer and adolescence; black bile was dry and cold like autumn and midlife, and phlegm was cold and humid like winter and old age. In the course of life a person slowly changed his or her temperament, although some dominant characteristics remained the same.

Foods were characterized in this way as well. In case of illness, the balance between the humors was disturbed by external causes, which could be treated by foodstuffs of the opposite quality. For example, if someone was suffering from influenza and had too much cold and humid phlegm, he should be cured with food and drink of dry and warm qualities, such as warm wine with spices. We find this clearly in the recipes. Fish, for example, was also thought to be cold and humid. This quality needed to be balanced in the preparation (by boiling the fish, or by spit roasting) and by adding a sauce or seasoning with warm spices.

Now that I have set the stage and outlined to you the kinds of foods, medical methods and recipes that the Dutch used in the Netherlands, let's look at what happened when they came to America.

Those practical merchants who formed the West India Company intended that the colony be not only self-sufficient, but also able to provision the company's officials and ships engaged in the fur trade and the trade with the West Indies. The settlers brought fruit trees such as apples, pears and peaches; and seeds for vegetables such as lettuces, cabbages, parsnips, carrots or beets and for herbs like parsley, rosemary, chives or tarragon. Farm animals such as horses, pigs or cows were also brought here. Aboard ship they had their own stalls and often each had an attendant, who would get a bonus when the animal arrived safely.

The new land was very fertile. Jacob Steendam, one of the three major Dutch-American poets of New Netherland, called the colony "a land of milk and honey." Adriaen van der Donck, who wrote *A Description of New Netherland*, published in 1655 to entice his fellow countrymen to come and settle in the new colony, was also impressed with its fertility. He reported that by the middle of the seventeenth century all sorts of European fruits and vegetables "thrive well," and he marveled at the native fish, fowl and other wildlife that was available in great abundance.

Trade with the Native Americans was an important aspect of life in New Netherland. The Dutch traded cloth, beads and ironware such as brass kettles for beaver skins. In the more elaborate explanation of Native American food ways in Chapter 4, you'll see that these kettles had a great impact on Native American food preparation. They eventually replaced the earthenware pots that had been used prior to Dutch arrival.

The Dutch also used their baking skills to produce breads, sweet breads and cookies to trade with the Native Americans. The natives valued the wheat bread of the Dutch because wheat had been unknown to them. Harmen Meyndertsz van den Bogaert, a surgeon at Fort Orange who kept a diary of his journey to Mohawk and Oneida country, related in his diary of 1634–35 that when he was more than a day's walk away from the fort, a Mohawk Indian who had just come from there offered him a piece of wheat bread. An ordinance for Fort Orange and the village of Beverwijck (now Albany) forbade such baking of bread and cookies for the natives. Evidently the bakers were using so much flour for this trade that not enough was left to bake bread for the Dutch community. Noting this regrettable state of affairs, the ordinance commanded the bakers to bake bread twice a week for the settlers. There is even a record of a court case in which the baker is fined because "a certain savage" was seen coming out of his house at a time of grain scarcity "carrying an oblong sugar bun." (See Chapter 3 to learn more about bread.)

In their new country, the colonists continued to prepare the dishes they were used to. From ships' records we know that the West India Company ships brought the settlers necessary kitchen tools, such as the frying pans to fry their favorite pancakes or the irons to make their hard and soft waffles. The Dutch settlers tried to duplicate life in the Netherlands.

Although they continued their own food ways, they did incorporate native foods into their daily diets. They did so, however, in ways that were familiar to them; for example, when they made pumpkin cornmeal pancakes (cornmeal instead of wheat flour) or pumpkin sweetmeat (in stead of quince paste). For lovers of porridge, it was easy to get used to *sapaen*, the Indian cornmeal mush, although the Dutch added milk to it. This dish became an integral part of the Dutch-American diet. (See Chapter 4.)

Though the daily fare may have been frugal, as Peter Kalm recounted (we might say "griped about") in his diary of 1749–50, it was contrasted by real feasts for holidays, special occasions or guests. From Mrs. Anne Grant's *Memoirs of an American Lady*, published in 1809, we learn that "for strangers a great display was made." She was a Scottish woman, who described in her book her youth spent with the Schuyler family of Albany: "In all manner of confectionery and pastry these people excelled." In the recipe collection of the Albany Van Rensselaers, we again see that the old Dutch recipes for baked goods survived.

Although many descendants might have forgotten the native tongue, they did not forget the taste of the foods of their ancestors and continued to enjoy the pastries and other items connected with feasts and holidays—not only well into the nineteenth century, but also to the present day. Cookies, pancakes, waffles, *olie-koecken* (deep fried fritters, forerunners to the doughnut), pretzels and coleslaw are some of the items that were brought to America by the Dutch colonists. Vestiges from those original food ways can be found in the American kitchen today. The next time you have a doughnut for breakfast, enjoy the crunchy coleslaw that accompanies your sandwich at lunch or eat a cookie with your afternoon tea, you too will be perpetuating food ways brought here by Dutch settlers more than three hundred years ago.

Chapter 3

BEER AND BREAD

In 1996, the annual Rensselaerswijck Seminar, organized by the New Netherland Project in Albany, had as the topic "Bread and Beer." The information on bread that follows is based on my research for a paper given at that seminar, and I am most grateful to my colleague and coauthor, Dr. Donna R. Barnes, for allowing me to use some of the information in her paper on beer and taverns.

BEER

Beer was as important to the Dutch diet as bread. As in many other parts of Europe, men, women and children drank it every day at every meal. We see it depicted in the still lifes of the Dutch Masters, in which a glass of beer stands on the table with bread and cheese or flanks a simple meal of herring, onions and bread. In Jan Victors's portrayal of the orphans at the Amsterdam Municipal Orphanage, beer is paired with the evening meal of porridge (and bread). In this dairy country, milk was available, but without refrigeration there was no way to preserve it other than by making it into cheese or butter. Beer, made from boiled water, was safer to drink than the polluted water from canals and streams and had nutritional value as well. It was therefore one of the most important beverages. It was not until the very end of the seventeenth century and beginning of the eighteenth century that tea and coffee replaced beer in the diet.

Beer was not only drunk at home but also in the local taverns, which were important social institutions in which people gathered to slake their thirst but also to clinch a deal, as was the custom, with a handshake and a drink, particularly on market days. It was a place where one could learn the latest local gossip or the news of the war with Spain (the Eighty Years' War from 1568 to 1648). In the taverns, weddings were celebrated, but they were also spots to come and enjoy the music of an itinerant musician and sing along or dance. People gambled, played cards, watched cockfights and played skittles, bowls or trick-track, as period paintings show.

Each country village had its tavern, but a city such as Amsterdam had many, divided among the neighborhoods. Simon Schama says that in the beginning of the seventeenth century there were more than five hundred taverns in that city. In the country, taverns were established along well-traveled roads, so weary travelers could have a meal and libation, and especially along the canals used by horse-drawn barges. While waiting for their boats, passengers might have a drink and a meal, perhaps *doopvis* (freshly caught river fish that was dunked in its parsley-flavored poaching water and served with bread), which was so popular at the time, and a glass of beer (or wine) to go with it.

Beer brewing was a major industry for cities such as Haarlem, Leyden and especially Gouda, where at the beginning of the sixteenth century there were already 148 breweries in operation. Not all of that beer was consumed locally; the breweries sold it in neighboring provinces and as far away as Flanders. By the mid-sixteenth century, however, Delft had overtaken the others and was the main brewing town. The government levied taxes on beer and heavily regulated brewing practices, but nevertheless the brewing industry grew, particularly during the seventeenth century when the breweries in Haarlem and Rotterdam rose to the forefront and brewing became their major industry. Rotterdam had very good water and was therefore known for its good beer. In contrast, Amsterdam had polluted water and had to send boats—in the winter with icebreakers—to the river Vecht to get decent water for its brewing activities. Beers, like cheese, were named for the cities they came from, and each brewery, like today, gave its beer its own flavor.

What did that beer taste like? Other than the usual ingredients of barley or wheat and hops, beers were also flavored with fruit or herbs and spices. You might be familiar with the Belgian beers that are imported to the United States today with their additions of cherry or raspberry. These can give us an idea of how the old fruit beers tasted. Wheat beers are also making a comeback. The original beers were ales with stronger flavor, often cloudy and top-fermented at higher temperatures than lager beers. Some five hundred years or so ago, lager beer was invented in central Europe, which uses bottom-fermenting yeasts at lower temperatures. Those were the pilsner beers, some of which were imported to the Netherlands in the seventeenth century.

Children might have drunk a weaker beer than adults, with an alcohol content between 0.5 and 1.5 percent, and poor people might also have had to content themselves with the local weak beer. More affluent people drank the stronger beers and could afford to quaff imported brews from cities like Hamburg in Germany, Breda in the southern Brabant region or from Flanders. Just like today, people had their favorites.

The Dutch, as inveterate seafarers and traders, of course consumed beer aboard their ships as well. A list for "victualing" and rationing aboard ships for the East India Company warned that the fifty barrels of beer per one hundred men was "to be consumed during the early part of the voyage." It is added that for the ships that departed between April and November more water was to be loaded, "as beer does not keep long enough in hot weather." A separate quantity of beer was taken onboard to make a favorite porridge of bread and beer, a dish eaten by the general population as well and, of course, an ideal way of using up stale bread. The West India Company had similar lists for provisioning, ensuring an adequate beer supply for its ships coming to the New World.

Beer and taverns played a large part in New Netherland lore. There are many court cases found among the twelve thousand documents that remain from that period (1621–74) discussing brawls and drunkenness. Other evidence of drinking can be found in the glassware shards in archaeological excavations. Remnants of *roemers* with raspberry prunts (knobby protrusions on the stem of the glass, which helped in holding onto it when one had greasy fingers from eating, as customary only having a knife and hands) were found by archaeologist Joel Grossman in the block at the corner of Whitehall and Pearl Streets on Manhattan. Archaeologist Paul Huey found evidence of boxes with *pasglas* rings when excavating Fort Orange in Albany. The *pasglas*, a tall beer glass with lead rings on the outside, was used in taverns as a drinking game. The drinker was required to drink in one gulp precisely to the first lead ring—if he did not, he had to drink to the next one, etc., and ultimately pay for a new round.

Grains and hops were grown in New Netherland, ensuring a supply of local beer (and bread, as we will see in the next section). While there were West India Company farms on Manhattan, Jan Volkerts asserted in "Farming for Bread and Beer," a paper delivered at the same Rensselaerswijck seminar mentioned previously, that the "population of New Amsterdam, chartered as a town in 1653, became heavily dependent on the grain-growing areas on the mid- and upper-Hudson and on nearby Long Island." In the third quarter of the seventeenth century, agriculture flourished in the New Netherland area—by then in English hands—and large quantities of wheat were exported.

When Jasper Dankaerts came to the New World in 1679–80, he remarked in his journal (in the archives of the Brooklyn

This is a modern replica of a seventeenth-century *pasglas* with glass, rather than lead, rings. These kinds of glasses were frequently used in tavern drinking games. *Photo by Richard Jacobs.*

Historical Society) that in Albany and Kingston "they brew the heaviest beer we have tasted in all New Netherland and from wheat alone, because it is so abundant." Perhaps he particularly favored wheat beer because other grains, such as oats and barley, were used as well, both in the patroonship of Rensselaerswijck and on Manhattan. While a large brewing kettle was already present on Manhattan in the early 1630s, in Rensselaerswijck (present-day Albany County) people brewed beer privately, until the first brewer, Evert Pels, was hired by the patroon in 1642.

After Kieft's War in 1644 (see Chapter 1), monies were needed and the director general and council decided to tax beer at three guilders per *tun* (a *tun* is a large cask that nowadays usually holds 252 gallons). They also set the price for which brewers could sell beer to the tavern keepers at twenty-two guilders. In turn, tavern keepers were allowed to sell it to the consumer at nine stivers for a half gallon (a stiver or, in Dutch, *stuiver*, is five cents or one-twentieth of a guilder).

Beer, like bread, was also regulated. In a 1649 ordinance, during a period of grain scarcity, the brewers were ordered not to malt or brew wheat. Another ordinance forbade brewers to sell directly to consumers. A 1652 ordinance again prohibited the use of grain for brewing. The directive of 1655 pertained to the price that brewers were permitted to charge per *tun* of beer, which was set at no more than twenty guilders. The next year's ordinance set fees for brewing for private consumption. In 1658 again, the director and council ordered that beer be sold at fixed prices. These prices were set in silver (coin), beaver (skins) and wampum (called *seewant* or *sewant* in Dutch, wampum are white and purple shell beads used by the natives as currency; in areas such as New Netherland, where few coins were in circulation, they were a method of payment as well).

Beer and alcohol were used in trading with Native Americans. Henry Hudson and his crew discovered early on that Native Americans did not know how to handle the beverage and, unfortunately, the Dutch took advantage of this propensity when trading with them. Robert Juet's journal of the voyage of the *Halve Maen* (*Half Moon*), from April 4 to November 7, 1609, recounts that when the boat landed near what is now Albany, Hudson and his mate took some of the natives onboard and gave them wine and *aqua vita* (brandy): "In the end one of them was drunke...and that was strange to them; for they could not tell how to take it." Robert M. Lunny, the editor of Juet's journal, which was published by the New Jersey Historical Society in 1957, added a note that "[t]his intoxication was long remembered in Indian tradition."

Our friend, Dr. Kermit C. Smith, DO, MPH, an enrolled member of the Assiniboine Indian Tribe of northeast Montana and chief medical officer of the Indian Health Service (retired), told me, "There are no serious scientific studies but there has been at least one small study whose results determined that American Indians have a diminished presence or absence of an enzyme (dehydrogenase) that breaks down alcohol in the blood stream. The alcohol then circulates in the blood stream for a longer period of time having more pronounced effect in the brain."

Local ordinances in various communities and in New Amsterdam again and again forbade the sale of liquor to the natives, imposing hefty fines and later on even corporal punishment. They were totally ineffective, however, and Indians were "daily seen and found intoxicated," as one of these directives read.

While we now know that for some alcohol might be counterintuitive, Dutch physicians thought that beer was a healthful drink for the population of the Dutch Republic and its colonies. Physician Johan van Beverwijck recommended beer as a component of a healthful daily diet in his 1636 book. Amsterdam doctor of medicine Stefanus Blankaarts said that all that is made of good grains *is goed* (is good) and all beers made with hops are very good and healthful. As an interesting aside: he also used hops—hop shoots—in salads in early spring. He mentioned as well a strange-sounding drink that mixed wine and beer, called *koud schaal* (cold bowl), which he found to be not unhealthy if "eaten" in moderation. While he recommended Rotterdam and Haarlem beer, he felt that he should not disqualify the beer of the city where he practiced (Amsterdam).

So to celebrate its long and varied history, dating back probably thousands of years, let's have a toast to this old drink with a deep swallow of a modern wheat beer that tastes like a slice of liquid bread and go on to learn more about the great importance of bread in the seventeenth-century Dutch diet.

BREAD

Bread was the most important food from the beginning of the sixteenth century until the end of the eighteenth century, when the potato took its place. Before that time and with a much smaller population, the Dutch people were able to afford more meat. But when the population increased, meat prices were higher and people had to switch to the cheaper grains, according to Dutch historian Henk van Nierop.

The previously mentioned physician Stefanus Blankaarts began his book *De Borgerlijke Tafel* (*The Bourgois/Middle Class Table*) with a chapter on bread because he considered it to be *Koninklijk Voedsel*, or "royal food," and therefore, he said, it deserved to occupy first place. He listed wheat, rye, barley, oats, spelt, rice and buckwheat as the grains that he would talk about, not how they should be milled, kneaded or baked, but to explain their healthfulness. He gave the following advice: "Risen bread is better and easier to digest than bread that is not risen and all bread is better with its bran. Bread with hard or burned crusts is not good for you and bread that is not fully baked is harmful. But, truly harmful is bread made from wet, moldy, musty or wormy grains; you cannot make a new dress out of a threadbare one." He also found that fresh bread is better than stale bread, but it needed to have cooled before eating. He urged his reader to eat a lot of bread because "dishes will be improved by it." It was more healthful to eat bread that you made yourself because bakers were out for a profit and therefore baked inferior bread just good enough to sell. The following four paragraphs are my translation and sum up his other admonishments on bread:

> *Wheat bread is lighter to digest than rye, but those, who are very hungry or constantly hungry, are better off eating rye bread than wheat bread. Wheat bread with bran is better than white bread. White bread causes constipation and bread without bran has little food value and makes for hard bowel movements.*
>
> *Mistelluin, or mixed bread made from half wheat and half rye may be eaten by all. Twee-bak [zwieback] or beschuit [rusk] is considered to be very good and better to use for porridge than white bread. Cookies with spice are better than those without.*

Waffles made from barley are better than pancakes, but all articles such as waffles, pancakes, white bread—as well as several others that Blankaarts mentioned, like refined breads made with raisins or spices with names such as *broeder* (Brother), *suster* (Sister) and *poffen* (puffs)—were likely to cause constipation.

> *Another cause of constipation is porridge made from flour, but when eaten not too frequently, it cannot do much harm. The same can be said of rice porridge or Spanish porridge. Egg bread, pan bread, or turned bread (bread slices soaked in egg and fried on both sides in a frying pan) are all not unhealthy. Rye bread gives good nutrition providing it is made from milled rye. It is better for workmen than for those who study and get little exercise. Spiced koek such as Deventer koek is good as well as all such sweet breads made with honey and spice. Rye porridge is not bad only for those who work; others who do little work will get sick from it. Barley, whether made into bread or cooked in milk is not bad food, but it is better cooked in sweet milk.*
>
> [He could not approve of] *barley porridge made with buttermilk. Oats are alright when cooked in dishes, but should not be eaten too frequently. Buckwheat is not as good as wheat or rye, but buckwheat porridge is good, if eaten in moderation, but baked with currants it is better and healthier.*

The above overview of Blankaarts's chapter on bread, which I translated from the 1683 edition reprinted in 1967, gives us remarkable medical and culinary insights. By looking at period paintings, we get an understanding of what the breads he talks about look like. In *The Baker* by Job Berckheyde (1630–1693), we see a nice variety of baked goods. In the foreground, there are floor breads, so called because they are baked on the floor of the oven, as required by government regulations in two different sizes, here perhaps six and twelve pounds. The basket is filled with white, whole wheat and raisin rolls, rusk-like *zotinnekoecken* and pretzels. More pretzels are on the counter and hang on the multipegged rack, the customary place to hang *krakelingen*, which were sweet and rather dry hard pretzels, not like the salty

Job Berckheyde's *The Baker.* A baker blows on an animal horn (a means of communication) to announce to his customers that his wares are ready for sale. Shown in the foreground are two breads of different weight, a basket of rolls and, on the ledge on the right, portioned rolls called *schootjes.* A multipegged rack holds sweet pretzels. *Courtesy Worcester Art Museum, Worcester, Massachusetts. Gift of Mr. and Mrs. Milton P. Higgins.*

pretzels now sold on the streets of New York City. A period recipe called for a pound of flour and a pound of sugar, butter, eggs, cinnamon and potash (baking soda) to make these popular snacks, which, because they are rather dry, would keep for a long time and are best when dunked in some liquid. They were baked in New Netherland, as well, because they are mentioned in a bakers' petition of 1653.

The *zotinnekoecken* (in the middle back of the basket) are so called in the southern province of Brabant, while the same baked good is called *carsteling* in the city of Gouda and *eyerschotel* (egg bowl) in the northern province of Friesland. They get their bowl shape by being scalded in boiling water. After scalding, they are slashed on the bottom, baked in a hot oven and sealed with clay—a tricky job even for professional bakers. Apparently, they were so tricky to make that they are not produced anymore.

Other items portrayed are additional floor breads on a shelf behind the baker. Above them stands a brass milk jug, and next to the baker we find a bowl, which might contain a sponge (a small portion of risen dough) for the next batch of breads. On the ledge beside the basket are *schootjes*, portioned rolls. In another painting of a baker by Jan Steen, we see *halsjes*, attached rolls that are hamburger roll look-alikes. Still lifes often portray rolls with ends that show where they had been attached. Paintings of richly laden tables usually contain white rolls with a hard crust, slashed in the middle with little pointed ends. Some of the rolls are broken in half and show the inside of well-baked bread that would make any baker proud. Paintings by Clara Peeters, one of few female Dutch seventeenth-century painters, often show hardtack next to rolls and *zotinnekoecken*. Hardtack, twice-baked sea biscuits that keep for months, sometimes years, was the kind of bread used on ships. An ordinance of 1647 sets the rations for the West India Company ships as follows: "stew according to circumstances; 3-½ pounds of hard tack; 1-½ gills of vinegar; 1 pound of dried fish; and 2-½ pounds of pork or beef." These rations conform more or less to those of the East India Company.

In one of Cornelis Dusart's drawings (shown in Chapter 6), the girl on the right holds a large diamond-shaped holiday bread called a *duivekater*. The shape of these breads differed from town to town. It is a rich, buttery, often lemon-flavored white bread. Bread made from white (sifted whole wheat) flour was considered a special treat, as it was more expensive than regular whole grain breads. *Duivekaters* were dispensed to the poor by the deacons of the Reformed Church in Brooklyn on New Year's Day 1664, so we know they were made in New Netherland as well. Period art aids immeasurably in understanding the wide variety of breads available to the seventeenth-century Dutch.

What ties bread and beer even more together than sharing grain as a common ingredient is yeast. Blankaarts said in his first of eight rules about bread that it should be properly risen with the use of yeast or sourdough, as that is more healthful than dough that is not properly risen. What we now know as the "sourdough" method was the early way of leavening bread. A portion of previous dough was set aside to ferment and used to leaven the next batch, as you can see in the painting by Job Berckheyde. A natural byproduct of beer brewing is yeast, and brewer's yeast was used for bread baking in the seventeenth century Dutch Republic. The same method is likely to have been followed in New Netherland. According to an Amsterdam ordinance of 1652, the yeast for bread baking had to be unadulterated, just the way it came from the brewery, and measured with a verified and approved measure. In Leyden in the middle of the seventeenth century, yeast was sold in a *gist-huis*, or "yeast-storage house," but numerous petitions made clear that the bakers preferred to obtain their yeast directly from the brewery. In Dutch this period is called the *gist-twist* or "yeast-quarrel."

Bakers generally use a pinch of salt in their dough to control the rising action of yeast. (See my discussion of the salt trade in Chapter 9.) Yeast, salt, grain and water are the common ingredients of bread dough. I discussed in the beer section how water was polluted in the seventeenth century and that good water made for good beer. The same can be said for bread.

Bread grain was not locally grown—the wet, clay grounds of the Netherlands are not suitable—but imported from the Baltic states. Amsterdam had become an important transit market; in the first half of the seventeenth century, 50,000 *last* (roughly 120,000 tons) of grain were brought to Amsterdam, where they were traded. The prices set in Amsterdam influenced those on other less important regional markets. Most of the grain was used to feed the local population, and the rest was traded to France, Northern Spain and Portugal. Some wheat was grown locally, the province of Zeeland having been known since the Middle Ages for the quality of its wheat. The drier eastern provinces of Drenthe, Overijssel, Gelderland and the southern provinces of Brabant and Limburg grew mostly rye, which requires less moisture and ripened earlier than wheat.

A study of the agricultural productivity of Rensselaerswijck by Jan Folkerts shows that from 1642 through 1646 the main crops were oats and wheat: "The prices of wheat and oats generally were in the ratio of 5 to 2, so in fact wheat was the leading crop in the patroonship." He points out that while the republic had become dependent on the Baltic region for its grain, "in the American colony a one-sided directedness towards the cultivation of grain" was seen.

In his subsequent paper, Folkerts studied grain production on the island of Manhattan (you might find that farms on Manhattan are a bit hard to imagine nowadays) and found that the area really depended on the grain production in the upper Hudson Valley region. "When a crop failed in Rensselaerswijck, as it did in 1639, this had severe consequences on Manhattan," he said.

In the Dutch cities, the baker purchased his grain from the grain trader and stored it in his attic. The rural baker would buy directly from the grower, a practice that was followed in New Netherland. There, as in the Netherlands, grain was ground at a mill as needed for a milling fee, set by the local government. An early privilege granted to the city of Haarlem in 1274 by Floris V mentioned the standard grain mill. The top part of such a mill can be turned as needed in the changeable winds of Holland. In

Cryn Fredericksz's plan of New Amsterdam, dated around 1626 and the earliest known, a mill was already present, and a mill was also shown in the same location on the Visscher map of 1651 (shown in Chapter 1).

The most important among the baker's tools is the cavernous wall oven, stoked by *takkenbossen*—fagots or reeds—that create the lively fire necessary to heat its bricks. A petition of the Leyden bakers' guild of 1685 asked to be allowed to burn reeds, peat or sawdust and buckwheat shells. Attached to this petition is a resolution that allowed the burning of reeds on certain conditions. In New Netherland, fuel was not this scarce. Van der Donck reported how the new country's giant oak trees, from sixty to seventy feet high, were not only used for all sorts of farming purposes, but also made "excellent firewood, surpassing every other kind." The baker's implements included an ash rake to rake out the fire prior to baking; a mop to clean out ashes; an ash pot to keep the hot coals; a grain shovel; sieves; a trough for mixing and kneading; a table for shaping the dough pieces; a scale for weighing; boards to place the dough on and cloths to cover it for rising; baking sheets for small breads and rolls; and a peel to "shoot" the dough pieces into the oven.

Bakery shops were but a simple extension of the workroom. Sometimes the shop was no more than a window to the street. In his workroom, the baker mixed the flour, salt, yeast and water into dough, which was then kneaded to the right consistency. Wheat dough was kneaded by hand; the heavier rye dough was kneaded in a trough with the feet, while hanging onto a rail affixed above the trough. Hands or feet were not allowed to be washed with soap but were cleaned with hot water and then rubbed with flour.

Breads were often flavored with the spices brought by the East India Company to Dutch shores, such as nutmeg, cloves and especially cinnamon; and they were filled with "sweetmeats" such as currants or raisins. An ordinance from as early as 1601 forbade excessive ornamentation of baked goods with gold, probably gold leaf. New Netherland ordinances forbidding the baking for the natives in time of grain scarcity often specifically mention breads with sweetmeats.

In addition to shape or ornamentation, each baker placed his own identifying mark—such as a circle with a cross, or a mark that looks like an asterisk—on the bottom of each bread. Housewives, who preferred to prepare their bread dough at home, gave their breads a mark as well before they sent it out to be baked, a service for which the baker received a fee set by the local authorities in the Netherlands and in New Netherland. The bread marks were registered as well. The Municipal Archives in Leiden still have a list of bread marks from the late eighteenth century, which included marks for bakers, but also for "Marya Jansdr van Sereyen, *huysvrouw van* Willem Willemsen (Marya, John's daughter van Sereyen, housewife of Willem Willemsen)."

After the bread had been weighed, was shaped, had risen and had finally been baked, a baker would blow on an animal horn—a common means of communication—to let his clientele know that it was ready for sale, as we see in Job Berckheyde's painting. The Fort Orange Court Minutes of 1652–60 show that the practice of bakers blowing their horns was brought to the New World. Jochem Becker Backer was summoned to an extraordinary session of the court called on April 12, 1653, because in violation of the ordinance he had in the absence of the commissary publicly blown the horn to sell white bread (in a time of grain scarcity).

It was not the bakers who set the price for their bread, but the local government. Part of the government's task was to ensure sufficient food to protect its people against famine. Consequently, the municipal governments in the seventeenth century regulated the size, weight and price of the different kinds of bread. Bread prices were established in relation to grain prices. Rye bread had a stable weight of six and twelve pounds, but its price would vary. This was called *zetting*, or fixing the price. For example, in Leiden in the years between 1596 and 1620, the price for a twelve-pound loaf fluctuated between 5 and 9.5 *stuivers* (1 *stuiver* equaled 5 cents). For white bread, the price would be stable but the weight would vary. This is called *rijding*, a term hard to translate but which indicates that the price moves up or down. Prices and weights were announced in bulletins affixed to prominent structures in town, such as church doors. The same was true in New Netherland, where, for example, an ordinance of October 6, 1659, reads that each coarse loaf of eight pounds shall cost "18 *stivers* [*stuivers*], counting eight white and four black wampum beads to one *stiver*."

In the Netherlands, the bakers were organized in guilds. These not only petitioned the government on behalf of their members but also had as their main purpose the regulation and curtailment of the bakers' trade. These restrictions were necessary to ensure an adequate market share for each bakery. To be a full member of the bakers' guild one had to be a citizen of the town, had to have completed a certain amount of training in a bakery and had to have passed the baker's exam.

In order to ensure that the bread was the right size, weight and quality, the government appointed *brood-wegers*, or bread weighers, and inspectors. The same happened in New Amsterdam. On October 13, 1661, two men were elected and confirmed as "overseers of the bread" and charged with the responsibility of ensuring that "the bread is made of good material, proper weight and well baked." Both in the Netherlands and New Netherland, bakers were fined for selling bread with short weight or for adulterating bread with extra bran, even sawdust, or other materials. Their practices served to keep the overseers on the alert to spot infringements of government rules.

I have found no documentary evidence of a bakers' guild in New Netherland, except for a petition of the bakers to be able to form a guild that was turned down by the Fort Orange Court on May 9, 1655. It is pure speculation on my part, but perhaps the West India Company did not wish to have competition for its authority. However, at various times, the New Netherland bakers did band together when petitioning their governments. For example, bakers in Beverwijck (now Albany) requested that it should be left up to them whether to use sweetmeats in their baking for the natives, and there are other such instances of requests for mitigation of the rulings.

Bread was the mainstay of the diet. Professor A. Th. van Deursen asserted that a poor family with two young children in the rural part of Holland, where they would eat little else but bread, would eat about five pounds of rye bread a day. If we assume that the children would eat less than a pound each, the adults would have had about a pound and a half or a little more per person.

The Amsterdam orphanage records also give us a good idea of the bread consumption of the working class. Coarse and fine wheat bread was reserved for the staff. McGants found that the staff ate a diet remarkably similar to that of the orphans except for quality and quantity: at least ten pounds of wheat and four and a half pounds of rye bread per week in addition to goodly quantities of other foods. This generosity led her to speculate that some of it was meant to be shared with family members or was sold by the staff on the side. Since the Dutch have always been known as big eaters, the staff may also have eaten most of the food due to them.

Janny Venema investigated the care of the poor in Beverwijck, circa 1650–1700, by the deacons of the First Reformed Church. Bakers such as Jochem Wessels, Wouter Albertsen and several others baked bread specifically for the poor. According to the deacons' records, the poor were always given wheat bread because wheat was the main grain of the Beverwijck area.

While in the Netherlands, the working class ate rye or coarse wheat bread, daily consumption of white bread was seen as a symbol of affluence, despite the health advice of the doctors. The well-to-do burgher class continued the same plain-but-plenty meal pattern of the orphanage staff but showed off its wealth in the different kinds of white breads on its table, which accompanied fruit, perhaps from gardens, as well as fowl or meat for a frugal but ample dinner. Blankaarts said, however, that too much white bread causes constipation and that is why the "white bread children" (I presume children who only ate white bread) had such deadly white faces.

Native Americans in New Netherland liked the wheat bread of the Dutch. Wheat had been unknown to them, and the bread made from it had a very different texture and taste than the boiled or fire-baked corn bread that was a staple in their diet. An ordinance for Fort Orange and the village of Beverwijck gives a clear picture of the impact of the Native Americans' fondness for Dutch bread on life in the Dutch communities in New Netherland. It made flour scarce because the bakers preferred to prepare baked goods for the natives, which was more profitable, to baking regularly (twice a week) for the settlers' community. In the following ordinance (translation), the original author is responsible for the "standard" note:

> [H]*aving heard the manifold complaints of the scarcity of coarse bread which the bakers, contrary to the ordinance...of October Anno 1659, do not bake twice a week...consuming, to the serious prejudice of the community, their flour in baking* Koeckjens *[cookies] and white bread for the Indians, without {standard} weight...everyone who follows the trade baking shall from this time forth twice a week bake coarse bread for the accommodation of the community.*

It is clear that coarse (whole grain) bread was as essential to the communities in New Netherland as it was in the Netherlands, so much so that it can be compared to the standing of rice in Asian countries. Not until the end of the eighteenth century, when bread was pushed aside by the potato as the main food of the population, did it lose its importance. By strictly regulating the availability, price, weight and quality of the grain, governments in the homeland, as well as in New Netherland, worked to ensure an adequate share for their people.

Chapter 4

BREAD AND *SAPAEN*:
FOOD WAYS OF THE DUTCH
AND IROQUOIS

N ative Americans have hunted in the New Netherland area for centuries, using flint arrowheads and spear points. Aside from hunting animals, the natives gathered their food. Their early cooking method was by stone boiling: rocks heated in the fire were dropped in the cooking pot to heat the liquid and boil the food. By the seventeenth century, Native Americans had already cultivated plants for several hundred years and cooked their food in earthenware pots set in the fire or, as some have implied, in pots hung over the fire.

When the first Dutch settlers came to the Albany area, they encountered Mohawks who, together with the Cayuga, Onondaga, Oneida and Seneca, formed a family of tribes that the French called the Iroquois, thought to have been founded as the "Five Nations" in the middle of the fifteenth century and joined by the Tuscarora tribe around 1729. They called themselves the People of the Longhouse, or the *Haudenosaunee*.

Extensive excavations of Native American villages in New York State have taught us a great deal about their agricultural practices. It was because of those practices that they moved every ten years or so as their fields became depleted. Through those regular moves, the finds could be easily indexed chronologically.

The area south of Rochester, New York, is unique in North America in that it contains an uninterrupted sequence of villages that date from prehistory to modern times.

The Iroquois call their principal crops of corn, beans and squash the "Three Sisters," possibly because they were cultivated together. Corn is sown in hills about three feet apart. When the corn is about four to six inches high, the beans and squash are sown: beans in every hill; squash in one out of seven hills. The advantage of cultivating beans and corn together is not only the fact that the beans can use the sturdy stalks for climbing, but also that the nitrogen left by the beans improves the next corn crop. Squash, with its broad leaves, keeps weeds away. Another advantage of inter-planted crops is that they are less attractive to pests.

There were at least forty different ways of preparing corn, including a corn soup that is still a favorite and sacred dish for Native American celebrations. The corn is scraped from the cob—a deer jawbone is commonly used for this purpose, as shown in a painting by Ernest Smith. The corn kernels were cooked in water with ashes. The lye in the ashes helped loosen the skins. The corn was washed after leeching and cooked again with some beans and perhaps venison or fish.

Corn was pounded in a wooden mortar with a long wooden pestle and sifted to obtain a fine meal that was used for bread. The bread was either boiled or baked in the ashes. Such bread is mentioned by Harmen Meyndertsz van den Bogaert in his diary. His entry of December 23, 1634, says that he obtained bread, some of it with nuts, chestnuts, dried blueberries and sunflower seeds baked in it. The coarser pieces of corn, left over after sifting, were added to boiling water to make a porridge called *sapaen*, a word found in a variety of spellings. Many Europeans in America comment on this custom of pounding the corn and using it for bread or porridge (*sapaen*). Adriaen van der Donck, who wrote *A Description of New Netherland* in 1655 to entice his fellow countrymen to settle in the new province, as the Dutch called it, reports that "their common food, and

Ernest Smith's *Woman Preparing Corn. Courtesy collections of the Rochester Museum & Science Center, Rochester, New York.*

Seneca corn bread and *sapaen. Photo by author.*

for which their meal [flour] is generally used, is pap, or mush, which in New Netherland is named *sapaen*. This is so common among the Indians that they seldom pass a day without it...We seldom visit an Indian lodge at any time of the day, without seeing their *sapaen* preparing, or seeing them eating the same." Contrary to the Dutch, who adhered to strict mealtimes, the Iroquois ate when they were hungry and might therefore be seen eating at "any time of the day." There was no set time for a meal. The food was prepared once a day and was available when wanted.

Another description of Iroquois use of corn comes from Mary Jemison, a woman of possibly Irish descent, who was captured by the Shawnee Indians at the age of fifteen. Native Americans would capture their enemies and give them to those members of the tribe who had lost someone. They in turn decided whether the person would be tortured to death or adopted into the family as a replacement for the dead. Mary was traded by the Shawnee with two Seneca women, who adopted her. She remained with the Seneca until her death, married twice—once to a Delaware Indian and the second time to a Seneca—and had eight children. She lived to about ninety, and at the age of eighty, in 1824, she told her story to Dr. James Seaver, who wrote a bestselling book, *The Life of Mary Jemison*, which is still in print. She recounted that the cooking was very simple and consisted of pounding corn in a mortar, then cooking it and shaping it into bread, which was baked in the fire. Her implements consisted of a wooden mortar and pestle, a small kettle, a few knives and a few bowls made from wood or bark.

Naturally, wild native plants were gathered in season, such as strawberries and raspberries or other fruits such as cherries, grapes or plums. Poke shoots were eaten along with Jerusalem artichokes. Oil was pressed from sunflower seeds, and a variety of nuts was gathered, such as black walnuts or the abundant hickory nuts. In addition to fruits, vegetables and nuts, the native diet contained meat from four-legged animals, birds and fish. Adriaen van der Donck remarked on the great quantity of deer. He said that *the deer are incredibly numerous in the country. Although the Indians throughout the year and every year (but mostly in the fall) kill many thousands, and the wolves after the fawns are cast, and while they are young, also destroy many, still the land abounds with them everywhere, and their numbers appear to remain undiminished.*

Van der Donck also mentioned black bear as a source of meat. Similarly, Van den Bogaert noted that in one of the villages he visited he encountered a black bear kept in a pen to be fattened and later slaughtered for a celebration, which was a common practice with the Northern Iroquois.

Fish and shellfish were also abundantly available. Along the Hudson we can still find large hills of shells left by Native Americans. Pearl Street, in lower Manhattan, is named for the mother of pearl in the shells. Shad returns each year to the Hudson. Hundreds of thousands of pounds of shad are caught

Ernest Smith's *Drying the Plums. Courtesy collections of the Rochester Museum & Science Center, Rochester, New York.*

Ernest Smith's *The Hunter. Courtesy collections of the Rochester Museum & Science Center, Rochester, New York.*

each year. The river was filled with sturgeon (now forbidden to be fished due to overfishing), and the waters of the Great Lakes and Finger Lakes have similar large quantities of fish. No wonder that Henry Hudson, when he first saw this area, called it "a beautiful and fruitful place."

The introduction of European plants, trees and implements had a major influence on the daily life of Native Americans. Arthur Parker, a Seneca Indian whose life's work was the research of the history of his tribe, says that the arrival of the traders with their brass kettles was a big event in Iroquois culinary history. The kettles made it possible to cook in large quantities, and because of their durability and ease in transportation, they gradually (but not immediately) replaced the traditional earthenware pots. By the middle of the nineteenth century, it was clear that much of the Iroquois material culture was disappearing and that they were adopting the European food ways. Fortunately, a large private collection of Native American implements was assembled and later donated to the Rochester Museum, now the Rochester Museum and Science Center—the same museum that conducted the archaeological digs at the Native American villages in the twentieth century. It also collaborated with the federal government during the Depression and asked Seneca painter Ernest Smith to portray the daily life of his tribesmen, as seen in the illustrations in this chapter.

Through the museum I came into contact with George Heron of the Seneca Nation at the Allegany Indian Reservation in Salamanca, New York. George Heron is not only Seneca (meaning "people of the hills"), but also sixth-generation Dutch-American. His Dutch ancestor was Peter Crouse, who was captured and, like Mary Jemison, remained with his captors. Heron belongs to the clan of the hawks. The Seneca clans are grouped and divided into two moieties (two basic groups that together constitute a tribe), one of which consisted of the wolf, turtle, bear and beaver clans, and the other of the deer, heron, snipe and hawk clans. Membership in the tribe is inherited through the mother.

George Heron is one of the few remaining experts on the traditional Seneca food ways. He grew up on the reservation and attended a one-room schoolhouse. When he went to Salamanca High School, "It was the first time I sat opposite someone who was not Seneca," he said. He said that the different ethnic groups got along just fine, but that among themselves they spoke their own languages of Italian, Polish or Seneca. Heron still prayed in the Seneca language at the start of the large communal meals that he prepared on the occasion of the annual tribal meeting or as a fundraiser for his church, the Jimerstown Presbyterian Church, which in the late 1990s had a membership of 65 percent Seneca and 35 percent non-Indian. He grew his own corn for the traditional dishes that are part of these meals. He called this kind of corn "Seneca corn." He had the seeds analyzed at Cornell University, where he was told that the variety dated back to at least the seventeenth century.

I was allowed to help him prepare and serve the traditional dishes of corn soup and corn bread for the annual tribal meeting. He also taught me a variation on the recipe for *samp* or *sapaen*, for which he first roasted the corn in a frying pan and then ground it. This gave the porridge a nice smoky flavor. The menu for these communal meals was quite extensive. Aside from corn soup and corn bread, it consisted of pickles made from cucumbers from his garden, venison from deer he or his sons had shot, turkey, fried salt pork, squash, green beans from government allotments, mashed beans, mashed potatoes, cranberries and fry bread. Fry bread, made from wheat dough deep fried in hot fat, probably has a European origin but has become a symbol of Native American food. I have had it on reservations all over America, sometimes sweetened with confectioners' sugar or honey, other times folded with a filling of hotly spiced beans. Heron taught me how to eat a "Seneca sandwich," in which a piece of fry bread is folded with a filling of fried salt pork and mashed beans.

These communal meals are an interesting mixture of native and European dishes and show at a glance what is left of the native food ways today. Corn soup, corn bread, squash, beans, venison and turkey are still enjoyed today as they were in the past. Cranberries and potatoes are, of course, native to the Americas but were not eaten by the Seneca in the seventeenth century. (In Chapter 10, I include the recipe for boiled corn bread that George Heron taught me.)

Now that we know what kinds of foods were gathered, hunted and cultivated by the Iroquois and how their food ways changed through contact with the Europeans, let's have a look at how some of those foods were adapted by the Dutch settlers.

Trade with the Native Americans was an important aspect of life in New Netherland. The Dutch used products such as cloth and metalware such as knives, hatchets or the aforementioned brass kettles for trade with Native Americans. They also used their baking skills to produce breads, sweet breads and cookies for such barter.

The Dutch adapted some of the foodstuffs of the new country to their diet. As you might expect, they used them in ways familiar to them. For example, they made pumpkin cornmeal pancakes, pumpkin sweetmeat and in later years put cranberries instead of the usual raisins and apples in their favorite *olie-koecken*. Since they loved porridge, it was easy to get used to *sapaen*, the Iroquois' corn mush, although they added milk to it. It became a daily dish for the Dutch as it had been for Native Americans. In his 1749 diary, botanist Peter Kalm related that "in the evening they made a porridge of corn, poured it as customary into a dish, made a large hole in the center into which they poured fresh milk, but more often buttermilk. They ate it taking half a spoonful of porridge and half of milk...This was their supper nearly every evening."

Other sources, such as the nineteenth-century descriptions and illustrations by Rufus Grider, held by the New York State Library, also recounted that this Native American dish, with the European addition of milk, remained a favorite with the Dutch. As late as 1888, Rufus Grider reported that the descendants of the Dutch settlers in the Schoharie Valley ate a mush and milk dish, which he calls *sapahn*. In general we can say that, aside from those few adaptations, the colonists continued to prepare the dishes that they were used to and tried to duplicate life in the Netherlands in New Netherland.

Chapter 5

TASTE OF CHANGE

The descendants of the New Netherland settlers continued to follow their ancestors' preparation methods and food customs. Their recipes are found in handwritten cookbooks spanning more than three centuries. Further, as diaries and inventories show, the implements used for cooking those familiar foods cultivated in the New World were brought along as well. For example, the inventory of the estate of Margareta van Slichtenhorst Schuyler (1630–1711) revealed that she owned several copper and brass kettles, a copper skimmer, a copper *poffer* pan and a wafer iron. (A *poffer* pan has small indentations and is used in making *poffertjes*, the Dutch version of silver dollar pancakes; see illustration in Chapter 2.) Some of these items can still be found in the historic Dutch houses in the Hudson Valley that are now museums.

Two practically simultaneous accounts demonstrate that Dutch descendants continued to cook in the manner of their forebears. Washington Irving, himself not of Dutch descent but surrounded by Dutch-American in-laws and friends, drew a vivid picture of the good life of comfortable descendants of Hudson Valley Dutch settlers. Here is his appealing description of their hospitable tables in *The History of New York* (1809):

The tea table was crowned with a huge earthen dish, well stored with slices of fat pork, fried brown, cut up into mouthfuls, and swimming in doup or gravy…Sometimes the table was graced with immense apple pies, or saucers full of preserved peaches and pears; but it was always sure to boast an enormous dish of balls of sweetened dough, fried in hog's fat and called dough nuts, or oly koeks —a delicious kind of cake, at present, scarce known in this city, excepting in genuine Dutch families; but which retains its preeminent station at the tea tables in Albany.

Anne Grant, a Scot, agrees with Irving's account in her book, *Memoirs of an American Lady*, which is of the same year and is full of marvelous tales of Hudson Valley hospitality. This is her report of the generously laden tea table (keep in mind that by 1809 tea instead of beer was the common drink):

Tea here was a perfect regale; accompanied by various sort of cakes unknown to us [perhaps she is referring to *olie-koecken*]…*cold pastry, and great quantities of sweetmeats and preserved fruits of various kinds, and plates of hickory and other nuts ready cracked. In all manner of confectionery and pastry these people excelled.*

Recipes for the above-described delicacies were exchanged among friends and family and handed down through the generations, as remaining handwritten manuscript cookbooks prove. I have so far found almost forty such cookbooks belonging to the Dutch families of former New Netherland. In addition, I found another ten or so handwritten books of Hudson Valley families not of Dutch descent. These contained no, or at best one or two, Dutch recipes; for example, Eliza Cruger's book in the archives of Boscobel in Garrison, New York, contains a recipe for "Crulla," an anglicized form of the Dutch word *krullen*, or curls, which became America's crullers.

All of these manuscripts not only provide an impression of what the Dutch ate, but also serve as indications of social customs. For example, the appearance of a recipe for "Condale," an anglicized version of the Dutch *Kandeel*, in three of the manuscripts demonstrates that the old Dutch custom of celebrating the birth of a child with this special drink of wine and eggs continued here well into the nineteenth century. Maria van Rensselaer's recipe for *doot coekjes*, literally "dead cookies" or funeral biscuits, reveal another ancient custom. For funerals, biscuits as large as saucers were prepared. Fifty pounds of flour, twenty pounds of sugar and ten and a half pounds of butter make three hundred cookies, the recipe says. Harriet Bowers Mumford Paige of Schenectady, writing in her diary about a Dutch funeral in 1789, described the practice as follows: "It was the custom then at funerals to have cake & spiced wine & cold wine & pipes and tobacco—This afterwards shortly went out of fashion—not very soon however—The sugar cakes made for that occasion were large as a tea plate & they had a two bushel basket full."

I might interject here that finding the diary at the Schenectady Historical Society's archives was one of those exciting occasions that research offers. I had read the recipe in the morning in Albany, at Maria van Rensselaer's former home, Cherry Hill, and then read the diary in the afternoon in Schenectady. Harriet Paige's account immediately solved my questions about the recipe by indicating that the "sugar cakes" were as big as a tea plate, and therefore fifty pounds of flour would make "only" three hundred cookies. I have made these cookies, and they are not very tasty but improve quite a bit when dunked (a common practice) in sweetened wine, for which conveniently the next recipe in Van Rensselaer's book gives the directions.

From some of the families, only a single book remains. One such manuscript belonged to the Lefferts family of Brooklyn; another is that of Elizabeth Ann Breese, which, although dated 1805, contained some recipes that might predate 1769. Not surprisingly, the Van Cortlandt family, the Van Rensselaer family

A recipe for *doot coekjes* in Maria van Rensselaer's handwritten cookbook. *Courtesy Historic Cherry Hill Collections, Albany, New York.*

and the Dutch families in the New Paltz area have left the richest assortment. There are five Van Cortlandt manuscripts. The oldest book belonged to Anna de Peyster (1701–1774), a maternal aunt of Pierre van Cortlandt. She gives recipes for *puffert* (a raised puffed pancake); hard and soft waffles; and *bollebuysjes* (an old name for *poffertjes*, silver dollar pancakes). We know from her estate inventory that she also possessed a *poffertjes* pan.

Another handwritten cookbook belonged to Anne Stevenson (1774–1821), wife of Pierre van Cortlandt II, and her mother Magdalena Douw (1750–1817). Her cookbook contained two recipes for *olie-koecken*, as well as recipes for waffles, hard and soft, *bollabouche* (yet another word for *poffertjes*) and pancakes.

The Van Rensselaer family was amazingly prolific in their record keeping. There are twelve handwritten books of five generations, spanning almost two hundred years. Maria van Rensselaer's is the first; her daughter Arriet's survived, as did those of Arriet's daughters, Elizabeth, Matilda, Harriet and Catherine; followed by those of Harriet's daughter, also named Harriet; and her cousin Catherine's daughter, Emily Rankin, who represented the fifth generation and was the last owner of Cherry Hill, the ancestral home in Albany.

Manuscripts also survived of lesser known families. Mrs. Anna Maria Elting's manuscript was dated May 8, 1819. In beautiful handwriting it recorded many recipes, including more than a dozen that are typically Dutch. Eventually the manuscript showed a different hand, and recipes are dated 1849 and 1850, but even in that period some recipes are Dutch-American. "Hylah Hasbrouck's Receipts," dated 1840, counted among them a recipe for "Condale," an anglicized form of *Kandeel*, and I found the same recipe in an unidentified book dated July 5, 1849. The book of Jemima Schoonmaker of Kingston, Ulster County, contained a poem dated March 3, 1813, and another of January 1832, as well as loose clippings, mementos and lots of recipes, many Dutch-American favorites among them. (In Chapter 10, four of the recipes from the handwritten books are included.)

Aside from manuscript cookbooks, recipes can also be found among other papers or in diaries and journals. Washington Irving's journals contained two recipes for crullers, and Huybertie Pruyn of Albany had several recipes among her papers.

Not only handwritten sources show us that the Dutch descendants retained their culinary ethnicity by handing down

Recipes for hard and soft *Wafels* (wafers and waffles) from the De Peyster Van Cortlandt papers. *Courtesy Historic Hudson Valley, Tarrytown, New York.*

their special recipes; church cookbooks of the late nineteenth century present the same picture. Good examples are *Old Dutch Receipts*, published in 1885 by the Lafayette Reformed Church of Newark, and *Crumbs of Comfort* (my favorite title!) by the Young Ladies Mission Band of the Madison Avenue Reformed Church of Albany of the same year. In *Famous Old Receipts* of 1906, Mrs. Francis Taylor Chambers shared her great-grandmother Elizabeth van Rensselaer's recipe for *olycooks*. Community cookbooks also reflect the participation of

Dutch descendants, as we learn from the New Paltz *Keukenboek*, or "Kitchen Book," of December 1909; the book of the town of Hurley called *Keukenkas*, or "Kitchen Cupboard," of 1959; and *The Helderberg Housewife* of 1967, a slim volume filled with wonderful old Dutch-American dishes.

In this span of 350 years, the recipes change, partially because the fine details of the methods were forgotten, but also because new equipment came along or new ingredients were invented. Not only did the recipes change, but their names also became more and more anglicized. *Krullen*, Dutch for curls, a deep-fried pastry, became "krullens" and then "crulla," which changes into "crullar" and finally ends up as "cruller." In "The Legend of Sleepy Hollow" (1820), Irving describes it as the "crisp and crumbling cruller," which gives a good clue that in the early nineteenth century this pastry was still, like its Dutch original, a thin, flaky, indeed quite easily crumbled, corkscrew-shaped pastry, not the soft, cakelike, twisted doughnut of today.

In the handwritten books, waffles are frequently spelled still in the Dutch way as *wafels*; they are often separated in recipes for soft *wafels*, the raised variety, and hard *wafels*, which are wafers. Another good example is coleslaw. The origin of this cabbage salad is apparently completely forgotten, because many strange stories are written about it. Even in the nineteenth century, housewives mistakenly called it "cold slaw," and it got a counterpart in "hot slaw"; yet the name comes simply from the Dutch *kool* for cabbage, and *sla* for slaw or salad. In 1749, Peter Kalm wrote in his diary that his Dutch landlady, Mrs. Visher, served him an "unusual salad" of cabbage cut into thin strips of one-sixteenth of an inch wide and mixed with oil, vinegar, salt and pepper. He commented that "it tasted better than one can imagine." America has been eating coleslaw ever since.

Other variations in spelling occurred over the years. In a conversation, Dr. Charles T. Gehring, director of the New Netherland Project, told me that the Dutch word *koek* (generally referring to a flat and not highly risen baked good) and its diminutive *koekje* (or, in seventeenth-century Dutch, *koeckje* or *koeckjen*) form the root of the American word cookie. He told me that it is quite possible that early Dutch settlers pronounced *koekje* as *koekie* (which sounds just like cookie in English) since the "ie" diminutive was a dialectal variation in the seventeenth century and is still a feature of western Dutch dialects. The word *koekje* in various spellings is also used for small items fried in a *koekepan*, or pancake pan, and for any small sweet morsel, like candied quince squares, which are called in Dutch *quee-koeckjes*, or "quince cookies."

The widest variety of spellings I found was for the seventeenth-century *olie-koecken*, or oil cakes, a word that has even changed in the Netherlands, as the pastry is now called *oliebollen* or oil balls. The Dutch-American spelling ranges from *oelykoeks* or *ollykoeks* to *ole cook* and *oly cook*, as Irving calls them. In his honor and as a result of his immensely popular book, *A History of New York, by Diedrich Knickerbocker* (a parody written by Washington Irving), these deep-fried fritters apparently also became known as knickerbockers. In *Cookery As It Should Be* of 1855, they are listed as "olecokes, or Knickerbockers."

The recipe for *olie-koecken* will be discussed in more detail because they became an edible symbol of ethnicity for Dutch-Americans. The recipe for these forerunners of the doughnut in the 1683 edition of *The Sensible Cook* calls for two pounds of wheat flour, not quite a pint of milk, "half a small bowl of melted butter," a large spoon of yeast, mixed with "a cup of the best apples" cut into small pieces, two pounds of raisins and six ounces of whole almonds, and this delicious mixture is seasoned with cinnamon, ginger and cloves. The dough is allowed to rise until light. The traditional preparation method, still used in the Netherlands, is as follows: a portion of dough is scooped up with a spoon, and this dough ball is then pushed off with the aid of another spoon into a pot of hot fat or oil. *The Sensible Cook* calls for rapeseed oil as the cooking medium.

Over the years, both the ingredients and the method changed. I have found few recipes that are as elaborately filled as the one in *The Sensible Cook* and not one that included almonds. I believe that the settlers did the best they could with what they had, keeping the spirit of the recipe intact. Since almonds and raisins were not so readily available, they made the dough itself richer by adding eggs and more butter. The "half a small bowl of melted butter" and no eggs in the 1683 recipe became a pound of butter and twelve eggs. The most common recipe for Dutch-American *olie-koecken* calls for "4 pounds flour, 1 pound sugar, 1 pound butter and 12 eggs, a teacup of yeast and as much milk as you please say near or quite 3 pints"—the way Anne Stevenson van Cortlandt wrote it. She marked it "Albany method," perhaps because she got it from a friend or family member in that city. In the manuscript of Maria van Rensselaer of Albany, the recipe is nearly identical, but she specified no further than "as much milk as you like." The Albany method is the typical New Netherland preparation of *olie-koecken*. It appears over and over again in various recipe collections. Eliza Tenbrook's *ole cooke* again called for that familiar combination of four pounds of flour, one pound of butter and twelve eggs. Another recipe on the same page divided the ingredients in half and suggested that some mace be added, but it still directed the preparation of *olie-koecken* according to the Albany method.

It is clear that more flour was added. Recipes often read: "flour to stiffen." This was done not only because all of the eggs and butter had to be accommodated, but also because the original drop method, which created a free-form shape, was either forgotten or abandoned in order to enable the insertion of a few raisins only to each dough ball. In *Some Remembrances*, (1928–29), Huybertie Pruyn Hamlin recalls that "it is said that only a Dutch cook can put the raisins, soaked over night in brandy, in the center." I have seen several recipes that call for a glass of brandy, which apparently was used to soak the raisins, and perhaps the cook had a little nip. It is not quite as much of a mystery as Huybertie Pruyn makes it out to be how the raisins got into the middle of the *olie-koecken*. Some recipes spell it out, and there seemed to be two ways of doing it. One was to use a broom straw to push the raisins into the center of the dough ball; the other was to pat out the dough, cut it into squares, place a few raisins in the middle and pull the sides up to make a ball. A common warning in the recipes is to "make them round." If raisins were not available at all, apparently other fruits were used. I have seen a recipe that used stewed apples, but the most interesting substitution comes from a letter inserted in a Van Cortlandt family cookbook dated 1865, in which it is suggested to put "cranberries stewed very dry" inside, as a true adaptation to the new country's foodstuffs.

Here the *olie-koecken* must be set aside momentarily for the doughnut, so that the two can be joined later. In the *History of New York*, Washington Irving mentioned the "doughty doughnut." Recipes for doughnuts generally sound quite frugal. They were made from bread dough, sometimes with the addition of a few eggs or some extra sugar. The chunks of dough were then deep-fried just like *olie-koecken*. In fact, recipes for deep-fried dough are universal; deep-fried dough of various kinds is part of the cuisines of the Middle East and Europe. What makes the American doughnut unique is that Irving's "doughty doughnut" and its Dutch counterpart, which he calls the "tenderer oly cook," come together to create what we now know as the American doughnut, a favorite breakfast and snack food.

It all happened because of the fact that in the middle of the nineteenth century the use of baking powder became quite popular. Cooks, used to slow-working yeast, were enchanted with its rapid rising powers and recipes were rewritten to use this new-fangled product. Although some of the Dutch-American cooks stuck to the old yeast method, I agree with the late culinary historian Karen Hess that "the change of form of the doughnut was imposed by the new baking powder dough." A yeast dough can be scooped up and dropped, free-form, into hot oil or lard, or simply pinched off and dropped into the hot fat, but baking powder dough needed to be patted or rolled out and, because it is less sturdy, needed to be cut into a shape. In addition, they are more difficult to cook all the way through: soggy centers are a problem. A logical solution was, therefore, to cut a hole in the middle. Hess, in her *The Virginia Housewife*, quotes an 1883 recipe that refers to a doughnut cutter. Further, Warren Liddle of Schenectady, in *Old Cookery Older Cooks* of November 1979, quoted an old recipe for crullers, sometimes a synonym for doughnuts, which required them to be rolled an inch thick and "cut out with a cutter that has a hole in the center."

In today's American doughnut, we inherit a combination of the rich, cakelike quality of the Dutch-American specialty, combined with the ready availability of the universal, simpler doughnut, mixed with the practicality of the baking powder age, made into a new pastry that represents the New World in a new way. The Dutch touch left a lasting mark on America's kitchen.

Chapter 6

THE SAINT NICHOLAS
CELEBRATION

The legend of Saint Nicholas is like an elaborate piece of embroidery with many intertwined threads, threads that start in the fourth century and wind their way through history to the present day, not only in Asia Minor and Europe, but also in North and South America.

He is believed to have been the bishop of Myra, present-day Kale, on the south coast of Asia Minor between the islands of Rhodes and Cyprus. He is said to have died on December 6, AD 343, or in any case between AD 340 and AD 350. December 6, as "Nicholas Day," is part of the Roman calendar. Saints' days are generally celebrated on the day of their death (and their rebirth in heaven). In Byzantine icons, Nicholas is portrayed as a bishop dressed in the vestments of the Eastern Orthodox Church, wearing an *omophorion*, the symbol of his spiritual and ecclesiastical authority. Originally of wool, it is a band of brocade decorated with crosses and is worn about the neck and shoulders. In modern portrayals, he is clad in the vestments of a bishop in the Roman Catholic Church.

Nicholas was the son of well-to-do parents, and according to the tales about him, he was already pious as an infant. On the

Saint Nicholas portrayed in cookie form. *Courtesy Historic Hudson Valley, Tarrytown, New York.*

fasting days of Wednesday and Friday, he would only suckle at his mother's breast once a day, just enough to sustain him. He grew up into a pious man associated with many miracles. I must point out, though, that the first encomium of Saint Nicholas (the description of the life of a saint) was written between 814 and 840, nearly five hundred years after his death, which explains the confusion in the details of his life and the hesitation of historians in pinpointing incidents. For example, Jeremy Seals mentions that although Saint Nicholas's life and that of Nicholas of Sion (the abbot of a monastery situated above Myra) are often confused, there is a reference dating to the sixth century that seems to confirm that they were two separate people, as Nicholas of Sion is said to have gone to the grave of Saint Nicholas in Myra.

Tales of Saint Nicholas saving sailors started to be told after the eighth century, and Nicholas churches appeared ringing the seaports of the Mediterranean, Aegean and Adriatic Seas. Sailors helped in spreading his fame. The practice of substituting Christian saints for pagan gods and Christian festivals for pagan ones has been encouraged by church officials over time. According to Charles W. Jones, this eastern saint is assumed to have taken the place of the Greek god Poseidon in the hearts of pagans. However, instead of causing shipwrecks, as Poseidon was wont to do, he saved sailors from them. Poseidon was also the god of horses and was purported to ride the "spume of the cresting wave" as if it were a horse, Jones says. Perhaps that is where Saint Nicholas acquired the faithful steed that we still see him ride in contemporary Dutch celebrations.

The Dutch tradition of Saint Nicholas bestowing gifts anonymously at night appears to hark back to the saint's most famous miracle. It is said that a poor father had no dowries for his three daughters and therefore decided to sell them into prostitution. Saint Nicholas heard the sad tale and came at night to deliver a bag or a ball of gold for the oldest daughter and returned twice more as the others came of age to bring gold for each of them. The saint is often portrayed with three gold balls as an attribute, and we see him portrayed in this way in frescoes and sculptures. Seventeenth-century Dutch painter Cornelis Vos (1584–1651) illustrated the entire miracle tale in "The Charity of Saint Nicholas," portraying it as if it happened in seventeenth-century Holland. On a dark night, Saint Nicholas is seen dropping a bag of gold through the window, while the three young women are busy with their sewing and lace-making and the father is reading. It is such a famous miracle that in medieval times it became an often-performed rhymed miracle play. Saints' days were celebrated on the eve of the day and *Sinterklaasavond* (Saint Nicholas's [day] Eve) is celebrated on December 5 to this day. The Dutch name *Sinterklaas* is a contraction of the words "Sint" and "Nikolaas" (Saint Nicholas).

Another famous story, later made into a miracle play, tells how Saint Nicholas saved three boys who had been killed, cut up and their body parts put into a pickle barrel. He restored them to life and punished the evil killer. The three boys in a barrel are also frequently seen in portrayals of the saint and even found on a Dutch seventeenth-century carved cake board.

In other stories, we are shown Saint Nicholas as a gift giver, whether of dowries or of life. I believe it is the purity of the anonymous gift, expecting nothing more in return than knowing one has done a good deed that has sustained the legend of Saint Nicholas. However, there is a pedagogical quality to his giving (perhaps another reason for his fame). It is illustrated by part of a song that Dutch children sang, and continue to sing, every year when Saint Nicholas Day was near: *"wie zoet is krijgt lekkers, wie stout is de roe"* ("good [children] get sweets, naughty ones get switches for spanking"), a sentiment duplicated in Clement Moore's famous poem "A Visit from Saint Nicholas."

The fame of Saint Nicholas spread steadily. Tales about him appeared in Greek texts of the ninth and tenth centuries. Around this time, Christian missionaries were sent to Moravia to Christianize the Slavs, and they brought stories about his good deeds. A Saint Nicholas church was founded in Kiev as early as 882. By 988, Christianity became the Russian state religion,

Saint Nicholas wooden cookie mold (left) shows the miracle of the three boys in a barrel, from which he restored them to life. The mold is placed by the hearth, together with wooden shoes, filled with traditional treats for Saint Nicholas's horse. *Courtesy Historic Hudson Valley, Tarrytown, New York.*

and Saint Nicholas was often portrayed in icons of the Eastern Orthodox Church.

Around the first millennium, pilgrimages (which would cancel guilt of sins committed) became very popular. Myra was on the way to the Holy Land, and pilgrims would stop to worship at the tomb of Saint Nicholas. Pilgrims were inveterate collectors of relics. One such relic might have been vials of the oily liquid that oozed from his tomb, said to have healing qualities.

On April 11, 1087, Saint Nicholas's remains were taken—or, one might say, stolen—from the church in Myra by merchants from Bari. On May 9 (Translation Day in the church calendar; "translation" meaning the removal/stealing of bones), he was interred in Bari in the province of Apulia in Italy, where he can be found to this day. Remarkably, the saint's remains continued to leak the alleged healing liquid when they were removed to Bari. Seals describes how he attended Translation Day in that city in the beginning of the twenty-first century, and the attending officials still collected the liquid from the tomb, which was seen as a sign of the saint's continued protection of the city. In Bari, Pope Urban II dedicated a basilica to him in 1089. By that time, Christianity and the legend of Saint Nicholas had spread throughout Europe from Germany to Russia, France, England and the Low Countries. The translation might have been the impetus of the Fourth Crusade (1202–4), during which western Christians turned against eastern Christians and even plundered Constantinople.

His fame was spread by returning Crusaders. Troubadours spread his lore as well, and he became the main character of medieval miracle plays and the subject of songs and hymns sung in the churches. From the start, he was a more secular personality, as he was never cloistered, and unlike many saints, he was not a martyr. He is seen to solve worldly problems, such as the lack of a dowry. He therefore became more of a folk hero, or an all-purpose saint, who is the patron of a wide variety of professions from button makers, solicitors, sailors and firemen to merchants, florists, tanners and, above all, children, scholars and schools.

Saint Nicholas came to the New World with Columbus, who named Saint Nicholas Harbor and Saint Nicholas Mole (a mole is a massive stone breakwater or pier to enclose a harbor) in Haiti. A slightly later explorer founded Saint Nicholas Ferry in Florida, which we know today as Jacksonville. But the more important story of Saint Nicholas in the New World has to do with the Dutch, and for that story we must turn to the Reformation.

Luther "denounced the mediation of saints as contrary to the teachings of the Bible" and taught his followers to pray directly to God. During the Reformation, as iconoclasts smashed paintings, sculptures and stained-glass windows depicting the saints, the celebration of Saint Nicholas moved from the church to the home, where gift giving now became central to the festivities. In the Dutch Republic during and after the Eighty Years' War (1568–1648) with Spain, stringent laws and regulations were introduced against saints' feasts and other Roman Catholic commemorations. Yet the celebration of Saint Nicholas Day, with its treats and gifts for children, endured.

In Dutch New Netherland, the present-day states of New York, New Jersey, Delaware, part of Pennsylvania and Connecticut, the fact that the celebration continued becomes quite clear when we look at a baker's account, dated March 1676, in the Rensselaer Manor Papers at the New York State Archives. Maria van Rensselaer, a member of the patroon's family, purchased a variety of Saint Nicholas "goods" (we could say "goodies") from local baker Wouter Albertsz van den Uythoff on an account that also included the purchases of *rusks, koeken* (probably a kind of gingerbread) and white bread. As explained in the chapter on bread, white bread was consumed by the more well-to-do circles or at special occasions. These treats were ordered for the celebration in spite of the fact that the Reformed Church in New Netherland, whose principles were upheld by the West India Company, had outlawed the celebration of *Sinterklaas*. A similar ordinance was issued in Amsterdam. As quoted by Jones, the ordinance meant "to take the superstition and fables of the papacy out of the youths' heads."

Descendants of the Dutch settlers continued to celebrate Saint Nicholas Day as their ethnic holiday well into the nineteenth century. Benevolent societies such as the Albany Saint Nicholas Society and later the New York Saint Nicholas Society held annual dinners on December 6. We have a menu for supper from December 6, 1830, at the American Hotel in Albany, which featured long-favored New Netherland dishes such as coleslaw, head cheese, sausage and *olie-koecken*, as well as *krulljes* (crullers), rather than the typical foods (mostly confectionery and baked goods) associated with the celebration in the homeland.

In the first fifty or so years of America's independence, holiday celebrations differed regionally, most New England Protestants still abjuring religious holidays like Christmas in favor of secular holidays like Thanksgiving and New Year's, while most people elsewhere observed Christmas and/or Epiphany as their major celebrations. In New York, meanwhile, the celebration of Saint Nicholas as a feast for children (*kinderfeest* in Dutch) continued, and New Year's was the big social occasion for adults. January 1 was the day when, in Dutch families, the gentlemen would go visiting and the ladies would stay home, dispensing caraway-flavored molded New Year's cakes with distinctly patriotic imprints, based on the wooden cookie molds used in baking the traditional spiced cookies for the Saint Nicholas celebration. It was a custom adopted gradually by other Americans as well. (See Chapter 7).

The transformation of Saint Nicholas into the uniquely American gift-giving figure we now know began with the publication of Washington Irving's historical spoof *A History of New York* in 1809, in which he describes Saint Nicholas riding the rooftops and "drawing forth magnificent presents from his breeches pocket." Jones asserts, "Without Irving there would not be a Santa Claus."

The name Santa Claus comes from the Dutch contraction *Sinterklaas*. I did not discover until very recently that to American ears, including my husband's (though he is used to Dutch accents), *Sinterklaas* when I say it sounds like Santa Claus.

Koekplanken. Wooden cookie molds for molding the traditional spiced cookies for the Saint Nicholas celebration One mold portrays Saint Nicholas, the other the typical windmill cookie that Americans know today. *Photo by Richard Jacobs.*

Not only the name changed, but also the saint's appearance: from a tall stern bishop he was transformed into a jolly, round, friendly Santa smoking a Dutch clay pipe. In nineteenth-century American postcards and illustrations, we see many incarnations until today's Santa—with his red outfit, black boots, belt and long white beard—finally emerged. Clement Moore's poem "A Visit from Saint Nicholas" (the authorship of which is sometimes contested), published in 1823, added the reindeer. By 1866, illustrator Thomas Nast built on the contemporary interest in arctic explorations and created a home and workshop for Santa at the North Pole.

Santa Claus, interestingly enough, was brought back to the Old World. By the second half of the nineteenth century, the English were becoming slowly acquainted with Santa Claus, who merged with Father Christmas, who had been imported from Germany, into one gift giver. In the Netherlands, however, the Dutch continue to celebrate *Sinterklaas* to this day.

Let's go back to the seventeenth century and look at the culinary treats that were customary at that time in the Netherlands and also in its colony of New Netherland, as we can see from Maria van Rensselaer's baker's account. Cornelis Dusart's colored drawing portrayed an extended family of parents, grandparents and three children celebrating together in their modest house. The grandfather sits close to the fire and smokes a pipe (note the filled stocking, which still hangs on the mantle), while the grandmother is still in her cupboard bed, smiling and gesturing at the wonderful treats that *Sinterklaas* had brought. The children are clearly overjoyed with their gifts. In other period paintings of the same event, such as those by Jan Steen, the children placed their shoes by the hearth. No matter what footwear was used, the children received presents.

The girl to the right near the well-worn broom has a basket full of baked goods on her arm, which includes a long, spiced *Deventer koek* (cake), but the basket also seems to hold a doll. The city of Deventer, situated in the northeast of the Netherlands, has been known for these spice cakes since the fifteenth century,

Cornelis Dusart's *The St. Nicholas Celebration. Courtesy Atlas van Stolk, Rotterdam.*

and they are still made there today. The child also proudly holds a *duivekater*, a holiday bread baked throughout the month of December at least until Epiphany or January 6. It is a rich, buttery, often lemon-flavored white bread (recipe in Chapter 10). As relayed in the bread chapter, *duivekaters* were dispensed to the poor by the deacons of the Reformed Church in Brooklyn, so we know they were made in New Netherland as well.

The little boy by the chair in the middle of the painting holds up a *kolf* stick. *Kolf* was played on land as well as on ice, when it was called *kolven op 't ijs*. It was played in New Netherland as well, for instance on the Hudson River when frozen in wintertime or in the streets of towns. Charles Gehring mentioned that there is an ordinance prohibiting *kolf* being played in Beverwijck because of broken windows and injuries to inhabitants. On the chair stands a shallow basket with more treats. It contains apples and pears, as well as more *koek* or bread. Various fruits, nuts and baked goods are associated with the *Sinterklaas* celebration, specifically seasonal fruits such as apples and pears, but also oranges from the Mediterranean area. Some think they were so well liked because of the popularity of the House of Orange during and after the Eighty Years' War. I speculate that they were given at *Sinterklaas* time because they resemble the golden balls given to the maidens without dowries. The legend of the "Three Maidens" did inspire the anonymous or surreptitious giving that is the essence of the celebration.

Spiced hard gingerbread dotted with whole almonds leans against the back of the chair. Recipes for both hard and soft gingerbread are found in handwritten cookbooks by descendants of the early Dutch settlers, passing along in this way the traditional recipes from generation to generation. The spices used in the baked goods, such as cloves, nutmeg, cinnamon or pepper, were brought to the Netherlands from the East Indies by Dutch seafarers. Russell Shorto describes in his book, *The Island at the Center of the World*, that when Adriaen van der Donck returned to New Netherland after a long stay in the homeland, he brought back one hundred pounds of pepper (for selling or bartering, no doubt).

The mother is lifting the baby for a good view of the festivities. The baby holds a *koek* or bread and on the floor are more treats, as well as a stocking containing a *roe* (bundle of switches, used for spanking). Since all three children seem happy, it is not clear for whom it was meant. All of these treats may very well have been purchased at the lively Saint Nicholas markets held during the weeks before the big day, where baked goods and toys such as dolls or *kolf* sticks were for sale.

Not all the well-known treats for the occasion are portrayed here, however. Associated with the celebration are *pepernoten* (spice nuts, known in America by their German name of pfeffernusse), small balls or chunks of spiced dough. As an extension of Saint Nicholas as a *huwelijksmaker* ("wedding-maker," by giving dowries to the three maidens), molded *vrijers* or *vrijsters* (male or female lovers) were baked from spiced dough. Young men and women would present these to each other as a sign of affection. Bishop's wine, a spiced red wine, is a usual part of the present-day celebrations.

Other items not portrayed include molded sugar animals and marzipan, still part of the celebration today. Johanna Maria van Winter explained to me that those items hark back to times before the Reformation when during church-imposed periods of fasting, such as Advent, the eating of four-footed animals (and their products) was forbidden. Marzipan was colored and shaped to look like sausages, and coarse fondant was poured into molds in the form of pigs, cows or horses. Professor van Winter, a medievalist at the University of Utrecht, added that in the Middle Ages saints' days were always celebrated on the eve of their day, hence the current Saint Nicholas celebration on the evening of December 5.

The intertwined threads of the legend of Saint Nicholas can be followed from the East to the West and from Europe to the Americas. The tales about his numerous miracles linger through the centuries, but what has sustained his image most is his unselfish, anonymous giving, a quality that was transferred to his American counterpart when Saint Nicholas became Santa Claus.

Chapter 7

THE DUTCH NEW YEAR'S CELEBRATION

When the Dutch settlers came to New Netherland, that vast area wedged between New England and Virginia, they brought with them not only seeds, tree stock and cattle, but also their well-established food ways and customs.

One Old World and New World Dutch custom was the making of congratulatory visits to relatives, neighbors and friends on New Year's Day. These visits became very much a part of social life in the eighteenth and nineteenth centuries on both sides of the Atlantic, but they went out of fashion in America in the early twentieth century; however, we know quite a bit about them. For example, John Ward of New York City wrote in his diary on January 1, 1861, that he and his brother Press (who insisted on making only "very few calls") visited 33 families. He and his friend Benjamin Church did better after the Civil War. Ward served in Virginia as captain of Company A of the New York Militia's Twelfth Regiment during that war. They called at 107 houses on New Year's Day 1866. Such a large number of calls required a strategy worthy of a military man. According to a carefully made plan, the two friends made their way from Washington Square on up to Forty-seventh Street, finding 71 houses open for receiving and leaving 36 cards at the others. His descriptions are quite complete. He remarked about eating plum cake at one house and talking about the incipient rain in Paris at another. He obviously enjoyed meeting the young ladies in the various families he visited. No wonder, a period etiquette book explained, "In receiving their company on New Year's day, ladies have the largest liberty and freedom. They can chat with any one who comes properly introduced, with the same frankness and lack of reserve that they would with their most intimate friends."

While the gentlemen went calling on New Year's Day, the ladies stayed home to receive. Gleaming silver and china were used for the tables, which were laden with the best the household had to offer. A New Year's Day in Albany (as elsewhere) was a happy but very exhausting one for the women, especially the lady of the house, writes Huybertie Pruyn about the period of 1885–92. Food was being served from eleven o'clock in the morning until ten o'clock at night. Male relatives and friends coming to visit meant an average of two to three hundred callers. She continued her explanation:

> *An extra man was stationed in the hall as doorkeeper, and messenger boys, newsboys with calendars, postmen, policemen and many others rang the bell and said 'May God bless everyone in the house and a Happy New Year to all!' Over and over we would hear this and the man at the door would hand each caller a paper bag containing four of the large nieuwjahrskoeks, stamped with flowers, figures, or the State seal, and filled with caraway seeds. In a dish were a pile of dimes, and a dime accompanied every bag [as a tip].*

According to the etiquette book mentioned earlier, the two or three days after the New Year's Day open house were calling days for the ladies, who would come together to toast the New Year and discuss "the number of their gentlemen visitors, the new faces they have seen, and the matrimonial prospects for the year."

For young boys, being allowed to go visiting was a rite of passage. In a charming book full of social history entitled

Grandfather Stories, author Samuel Hopkins Adams described New Year's Day in Rochester, New York.

"The fine flower of local custom was New Year's hospitality. On that day the Old Families kept open house with pomp, circumstance and a lavish prodigality of refreshment equaled today [the book was published in 1955] only by a gangster's wake." Everyone was welcome, and "dressed in their best bib-and-tucker" they would do the rounds, "eating their voracious way like a swarm of social locusts." What is most helpful in giving us an insight in the culinary aspects of such an old-fashioned event is Adams's description of what was served at various houses:

> *It was accepted as an article of faith that the Brewsters should serve five kinds of pie, including Marlborough* [a rich pie filled with stewed apples, lots of butter, eggs and cream]; *that the Rogers' chicken salad was beyond all competition; that the Stedmans could be relied upon for that meatiest of luxuries, scalloped oysters; that what was known as Charlotte "Roosh" attained its apex of delicacy at Miss Ada Kent's; and that the Pecks offered not only two kinds of turkey, but also duck and goose.*

But for young boys there was one house not to be missed because there they were treated to "exotic fruits and nuts," of which they were allowed to take some home, contrary to the usual practice (the best part).

While this book and John Ward's diary give an impression of how things were done in the cities, Isaac E. Cotheal, a gentleman farmer of Fishkill, New York, talks about New Year's Day in the country. In his diaries, which span some twenty-five years, he began each year with "a happy New Year to all"; he noted the temperature and the weather and listed who came to call that day. Some years he had as few as one or two callers, other years as many as eight. These are not quite the large numbers of visits that are possible when houses are in proximity to each other as they are in the city. One year, 1869, when "the day opened with a

Koekplank. A wooden cookie mold used for many different cookie shapes. *Photo by Richard Jacobs.*

heavy storm," which had not abated by 9:00 p.m., he recorded that he "received no calls."

The special treat for New Year's Day in the Netherlands was *nieuwjaarskoeken*, to which Pruyn refers. They originated in the eastern Netherlands and nearby parts in Germany. These paper-thin wafers were made in a special wafer iron, which left a different imprint on each side. The imprinted pictures sometimes had religious contents, such as the Crucifixion or the Resurrection; at other times they were of a secular nature, such as birds or flowers. Enormous quantities of wafers were prepared on New Year's Day, since they were not only consumed by family and guests but also distributed to children, who went from house to house singing New Year's songs, collecting their share as they went along.

In the New World, the character of New Year's cakes changed as time went on. Wooden cake boards, like the ones shown on page 98, now mostly held in museums or private collections, do provide the physical evidence that the New World adapted this centuries-old Dutch pastry. "New Year's cakes," as the cookies formed in these boards were called, evolved into uniquely American pastries by the nineteenth century.

How did a wafer made in an iron become a cookie to be rolled out and imprinted with a cake board? I believe that the American New Year's cake is a fusion of two Dutch pastries brought here by the settlers in the seventeenth century. The first is the *nieuwjaarskoek* described above; the second is *speculaas*, the hard gingerbread made from spiced dough formed in a wooden mold or cake board, in Dutch called *koekplank*, for the Saint Nicholas celebration. The smaller forms are now sometimes called "wind mill cookies."

Other Americans adopted New Year's cakes. Food historian William Weaver explains in *America Eats* that "by the end of the eighteenth century, when New York City served as the capital of the United States, New Year's cakes were in vogue among upper-class Americans, who imitated the Dutch custom of open-house visiting on New Year's Day." He also explains that their use was easily adopted by strict religious groups such as the Quakers and Congregationalists because the cakes were not connected to a religious celebration. An early, joking reference to the New Year's cakes occurred in Washington Irving's 1809 *History of New York, by Diedrich Knickerbocker*, where a "mighty gingerbread baker" received credit for being "the first that imprinted New Year's cakes with...mysterious hieroglyphics."

I believe that it was in the late eighteenth century that this homemade pastry prepared in heirloom wafer irons by one ethnic group—the Dutch—changed to a mostly store-bought product purchased by the population at large. They were often produced by bakers, who found it much more expedient to roll out dough, imprint it with a cake board, cut it and bake it. Therefore, the custom of serving New Year's cakes remained, but the pastry in its novel, new-country form became a thin, cutout cookie with imprint, baked to a pale color.

The cake boards developed into a unique kind of American folk art. Like the *speculaas* molds in the Netherlands, they recorded the events of the times. American cake boards depict political figures, the American eagle or the seal of the State of New York. A board by H.Y. Kelderhouse, dated December 12, 1867, showing a spread eagle with a banner reading "The Union Forever" is a perfect example of the patriotic nature of some boards. They

Above: Front view of large New Year's American cake boards, portraying American eagle and LaFayette. Private collection. *Photo by Richard Jacobs.*

Below: Back view of New Year's cake boards with carvings for smaller New Year's cakes. Private collection. *Photo by Richard Jacobs.*

were not necessarily only from the hands of Dutch-American carvers. Particularly well known was the work of Scottish carver John Conger, who worked in New York City from 1827 to 1835. Small, simply carved cake boards were for home use, and bakers also used the smaller carvings to have a variety of these cookies available. From the mid-nineteenth century onward, cake molds were even made in cast iron, specifically in the Albany/Troy/Schenectady area, known for its cast-iron products.

Recipes for New Year's cakes to be made in the smaller boards carved for home use appear in the manuscript cookbooks of influential Dutch families such as the Van Rensselaers, the Van Cortlandts and the Brooklyn Lefferts, among many others. In Chapter 10, you'll find a recipe for New Year's cakes, adapted from the handwritten nineteenth-century cookbook of Mrs. Maria Lott Lefferts (1786–1865).

The custom of baking New Year's cakes survived well into the twentieth century. Baker Otto Thiebe of Albany baked these caraway-flavored cookies until his death in 1965. This forgotten holiday of the past is inextricably interwoven in the fabric of American society and is part of the many contributions of the Dutch settlers who started a new life in the New World.

Chapter 8

THE PINKSTER CELEBRATION

O ur final holiday discussion is the celebration of Pinkster or Pinxter (*Pinksteren* in modern Dutch), known elsewhere as Pentecost or Whitsuntide, which occurs fifty days after Easter and is the third most important holiday in the Christian calendar, as it marks the descent of the Holy Spirit upon the apostles and other followers of Jesus. Jasper Dankaerts records in his diary of 1679–80 that on Pinkster he and his traveling companion Peter Sluyter went to visit the local church on Long Island and the next day, "the second day of Pinxter," they had several visitors. Visiting friends and neighbors was very much a part of Dutch social life, as you saw in the previous chapter.

Dankaerts and his companion came to America to found a new community for their fellow Labadists (followers of Jean de Labadie, 1610–1674, a French Jesuit who abandoned Catholicism and became an ordained Protestant minister). Dankaerts's diary is an important source of information on life in the former New Netherland area after the English takeover. In the end, the Labadists decided to settle in Maryland.

In the seventeenth-century Dutch Republic, the secular festivities associated with Pinkster were a kind of combined May Day and fertility celebration, in which a young girl was chosen as the *Pinxterblom* (Pentecost flower) and was carried through town bedecked with jewelry and flowers to foster a good harvest. In a painting by Jan Steen, the occasion looks familiar to us as children playing dress-up or going out to "trick or treat" on an American Halloween. The girl carries a cup to collect coins with which the children will buy treats afterward, and we see a bystander actually giving a coin to the *Pinxterblom*.

In the New World, the celebration took on an entirely different form. The eighteenth-century journal of Alexander Coventry related religious observances of the day, visiting among neighbors and the eating of colored eggs and waffles, always a favorite festive food with the Dutch. On June 4, 1786, he observed that "it is all frolicking to-day with the Dutch and the Negro…they have eggs boiled in all sorts of colors, and eggs cooked in every way, and everybody must eat all the eggs he can. And the frolicking is still kept up among the young folks, so that little else is done to-day but eat eggs and be jolly." It was a time of merrymaking, not only for the Dutch but also for their slaves, who got the day off. "The blacks as well as their masters were frolicking and the women & children look'd peculiarly neat and well dressed," says the June 6, 1797 entry in the diary of William Dunlap.

After the Revolution and in the beginning of the nineteenth century, the holiday became more and more an African American celebration. New York City, where freed slaves had arrived in large numbers, was especially known for its lavish Pinkster festivals. Historic Hudson Valley researcher Jackie Haley argues that this was the time that "African" churches and "African" benevolent societies began to blossom in the northern urban centers and a time when small communities of freed blacks were already established, which provided "the opportunity for an African identity and culture to gain ground and come to the surface." Descriptions of the nineteenth-century celebrations of Pinkster refer to its "African origins," especially visible in the dancing and the music of the drums.

James Fenimore Cooper described a Pinkster festival in his *Satanstoe* and remarked, "The traditions and usages of their original

Storyteller at a Pinkster Festival. *Courtesy Historic Hudson Valley, Tarrytown, New York.*

country were so far preserved as to produce a marked difference." He continued to describe what happened at the celebration: "Among other things, some were making music, by beating on skins drawn over the ends of hollow logs, while others were dancing to it, in a manner to show that they felt infinite delight. This, in particular, was said to be usage of their African progenitors."

According to historian David Cohen, "The celebration of Pinkster in Albany lasted a whole week," and he specified what it looked like: "Booths decorated with honeysuckle and may apple were set up on Arbor Hill. Beer, mead, cider, meat, fish, cakes, and fruit were sold, and there was also gambling and dancing." A prominent figure in the Albany celebration was a slave named King Charles, a "Guinea man" from Angola who lived to the age of 125. He is described in a poem by Absalom Aimwell called "Pinkster Ode for the Year 1803" as leading the "Guinea dance," dressed in his Pinkster clothes with "his hat of yellow lace."

The well-known abolitionist and women's rights advocate Sojourner Truth dictated (because she was illiterate) a book describing her life to her neighbor Olive Gilbert. It was published in 1850 as *The Narrative of Sojourner Truth*. She was born a slave with the name of Isabella in Ulster County, New York, in 1797. She later took the name by which she is known today. When she had left her master in New Paltz, New York, and was living elsewhere, she described how she thought of one of the festivals approaching. ("She knows it by none but the Dutch name, Pingster [*sic*].") As described above, the slaves would get the day off and "she saw retrospectively all her former companions enjoying their freedom for at least a little space, as well as their wonted convivialities, and in her heart she longed to be with them."

Although outlawed in places like Albany as early as 1811, apparently because of its raucous nature, Pinkster continued to be celebrated until the end of the century. In 1874, Gabriel Furman wrote, "Poor Pinckster [*sic*] has lost its rank among the festivals, and is only kept by the negroes; with them, especially on the west end of this island [Long Island], it is still much of a holiday."

Dancers at a Pinkster Festival. *Courtesy Historic Hudson Valley, Tarrytown, New York.*

All that remained Dutch were the name and the date of the holiday, as well as a flower in the azalea family named "Pinkster flower," so named not only because it blooms at Pinkster time, but also because it has the same light lavender color as flowers, though of a different species, called *Pinksterbloemen* in the Netherlands.

But Pinkster was more than a religious festival turned holiday; it eventually became a bona fide cultural event. In his article "Pinkster Carnival: Africanisms in the Hudson River Valley," Professor A.J. Williams-Myers of SUNY–New Paltz asserts that as a result of the Pinkster festivals, "for almost two hundred years some forms of Africanisms were able to survive within the institution of slavery in New York...These were passed on from generation to generation, from Old World African to New World African, so that by the nineteenth century Pinkster carnival had become an African celebration." Although long faded from practice, this forgotten Dutch holiday had a lasting impact on American life.

Historic Hudson Valley, with its executive offices in Tarrytown, New York, administers several historic sites. The Pinkster holiday is recreated at Philipsburg Manor in Sleepy Hollow, New York, with games, African American storytellers, music and dancers, as the illustrations show. (In Chapter 10, you will find a recipe for ginger beer given to me years ago at such a celebration. It makes a wonderful toast to spring!)

Chapter 9

CACAO, COFFEE AND TEA; SALT, SPICES AND SUGAR

In this chapter I will give you some thumbnail sketches of the important food-related commodities that were part of Dutch mercantile interests. These sketches are by no means comprehensive but will give you an impression of the vast trade activities of the Netherlands in the seventeenth century, and as you will see, the New Netherland or Hudson Valley area often played a role. Especially during the seventeenth century, these articles turned from luxury items into necessities for many European households. The only exception in that regard is salt, which was indeed an essential aid for food preservation very early on. I include it in this list because of the political, social and economic impact of its procurement during the Eighty Years' War (1568–1648).

CACAO

Cacao is the word used for the tree and its fruit/seeds, while the word *cocoa* is used for the ground and de-fatted seeds, as well as for the powder used for baking and the hot drink made from those processed seeds. *Chocolate* refers now to the beloved confection, whether in the form of candy bars, bonbons or countless other sweets. Confusingly, it initially referred to the drink made from the complete substance including the cocoa butter, which until the early 1800s was the only way cacao was used.

Common Stories of its Origins

Recent genetic studies have determined that *Theobromine cacao* had one center for domestication: South America, along the western slopes of Ecuador/Peru. Genetic studies of the tree in Central America and Mexico show that these trees originated in South America. Through the explorations of Christopher Columbus it was brought to Spain, and its use spread through Europe. A favored story often told is about Montezuma supposedly drinking fifty cups of the beverage a day, particularly before entering his harem. Another source says that he might have sipped just a little from each cup rather than downing each one. In any case, the implication is that cacao increased male vigor, a belief that carried over to Europe in later centuries, as we can see in Dr. Blankaarts's assessment below.

Varieties and Processing

There are two varieties of cacao: the *criollo* and the *forastero*. The first is considered to have more refined flavor and quality; the second to be more vigorous and productive. Cacao trees grow their fruit as large pods on their trunks and largest branches. The pods contain some forty seeds, referred to as "beans," surrounded by pulp. The pods are opened and the beans removed, after which they are fermented, dried and roasted, and their shells are removed by winnowing. What is left are the "nibs," which are ground into chocolate. The dried "nib" contains the delicious flavor we know and love, but more than half of the "nib" is the fat called "cacao butter" that we commonly call "cocoa butter." Up until the first quarter of the nineteenth century, the drink was made from grated chocolate, which had been mixed with spices such as cinnamon or vanilla and other things such as hot pepper and sugar, and then it was dissolved in hot water (later milk). It was not until 1828 that Dutch chemist Coenraad van Houten found a way to extract the cacao butter and create a less filling cacao (cocoa) powder, which he mixed with potassium or sodium carbonate so it would dissolve in water, a process called "Dutching." It made the chocolate flavor more delicate and the color darker. The thick, foamy chocolate of preceding centuries was appreciated as a very nutritious, stimulating drink.

Dutch Involvement in the Cacao Trade

The West India Company was not only involved in the fur trade in New Netherland, but it also had a firm interest in South America, particularly Brazil, and the West Indies. The Dutch wrested Recife from the Portuguese in 1630 and became heavily involved with the production of sugar. Even after the recapture of the Brazilian colony, they remained very active in the Atlantic world and retained Saba, St. Martin, St. Eustacius, the "ABC" islands of Aruba, Bonaire and Curacao and acquired Surinam in 1667. For the inter-Caribbean trade, Curacao became the local transit market for the Dutch, from which cacao was traded and shipped.

Period Comments

Stefanus Blankaarts, the influential Amsterdam physician, had the following to say about cacao in his book *Borgerlijke Tafel* (*Bourgeois Table*) of 1683 (my translation): "Chocolate is a very agreeable drink, also very healthful, and excellent in fattening a person. She is particularly good for people who just got married...because she makes good blood and juices [fluids]; and increases the seed."

Customs and Paraphernalia

Cocoa, or hot chocolate, became a popular drink by the end of the seventeenth century in our Hudson Valley area. From records at Fort Ticonderoga, we know that it was given to the soldiers during the American Revolution because of its nutritional value and stimulating qualities. The French Fortress Louisbourg in Nova Scotia, Canada, has similar records of soldiers getting chocolate (beverage) rations.

Hot chocolate was served in tall columnar cups. According to Amanda Lange, Curatorial Department chair and Curator of Historic Interiors at Historic Deerfield, Deerfield, Massachusetts, this is "to elongate the time that the froth survives—like the flute of a champagne glass—since drinking chocolate in the 17th and 18th century was all about the froth." It would be served from a chocolate pot with its handle at right angles with the spout and a removable filial to accommodate the whisklike implement called

A chocolate cup found at a Seneca Iroquois archaeological site (the Dann Site) dating to the period between 1655 and 1675. This cup might have been used as an item of personal adornment. *Courtesy collections of the Rochester Museum & Science Center, Rochester, New York.*

a *molinillo* that, when rubbed between one's hands (the way you do when warming your hands), creates a delicious foam. A two-handled chocolate cup of blue and white Delftware was found in a Seneca Iroquois archaeological site dating to the period between 1655 and 1675. Rather than for drinking, it might have been used as an item of personal adornment by Native Americans, as was often their custom.

Cacao in New Netherland

Since the fourth quarter of the seventeenth century there had been an increasingly important trade between New York and Curacao. Younger sons involved in Dutch firms were sent to the island to oversee mercantile activities there. Well-known Jewish traders like Daniel Gomez were heavily involved during the eighteenth century. Through the commercial activities of Frederick Philipse and his son, Adolph, who owned Philipsburg Manor in Sleepy Hollow, New York, there is a direct Hudson Valley link to the cacao trade. The Philipses' land produced foodstuffs not only for New York's urban population, but also for plantations in the West Indies, where preserved meats, dairy and wheat products were traded in turn for cacao to be brought to Europe for processing. Wim Klooster's book, *Illicit Riches: Dutch Trade in the Caribbean, 1648–1795*, contains lists that show cacao shipments from Curacao to the Netherlands between 1701 and 1755, ranging from 5,000 to some 485,000 pounds. In account books of New Paltz, New York Huguenot merchants, we find that by the 1760s cacao had become so much a part of everyday life that it was dispensed by the town to the poor.

COFFEE

Common Stories of its Origins

The origin of coffee lies in the Kaffa region of Ethiopia, from where it was exported to Yemen and Arabia. A favored story that pops up again and again in tales about coffee tells how a ninth-century goatherd noticed that when his goats ate the berries they were more active. He tried the berries himself and felt the same kind of stimulation. The oldest known Arabic manuscript on coffee dates to 1587. It proclaims to have been written 120 years after the drink's introduction in Yemen.

Varieties and Processing

There are two species of coffee plant, the self-pollinating *Coffea arabica* and *Coffea canephora*, which requires cross-pollination. At first the fruit might have been chewed whole or even boiled to make a kind of soup, but it was the Arabs, sometime after the coffee bean reached Istanbul, who cleaned and roasted the beans, ground them and stirred the ground coffee into hot water. It makes for a very bitter but stimulating drink. Its use spread through the entire Muslim region. Turkish coffee came into favor as well, a technique that boils the grounds. Cardamom was often added to slightly sweeten the beverage. Later, sugar was added.

Dutch Involvement in the Coffee Trade

It seems that coffee was introduced to the West by Italian traders. Alphoncius Pancius, an Italian scientist from the University of Padua, sent coffee beans to Dutch botanist Carolus Clusius (1526–1690), and in 1574, Clusius published a new edition of his herbal treatise, which had brought him fame, and included a drawing of coffee beans. The coffee trade in the early decades of the seventeenth century did not look so advantageous to the directors of the Dutch East India Company. Tea was easier to obtain, trade in coffee was entirely conducted by Muslim traders and the competition was fierce. Nevertheless, in 1621 a trade office was opened in Mocha and Surat, meant to facilitate the inter-Asian trade in coffee. Finally, by 1660, coffee was sent to the Netherlands, primarily to be traded to England, where coffee drinking had started in the 1650s and coffeehouses, the forerunners of gentlemen's clubs, were springing up. By the 1670s, such coffeehouses were seen in the Netherlands as well. A main event for the Dutch was the cultivation of coffee on the island of Java (Indonesia) by the Dutch East India Company in 1699. In 1711, the first load of coffee was shipped to Holland, and in one decade shipments grew from 894 pounds to 116,783 pounds. The English discovered around the same time that coffee could be grown in the West Indies.

Period Comments

As with tea, coffee was credited with all sorts of cures. An early Arabic manuscript even credits coffee with curing leprosy. Reay Tannahill, in her *Food in History*, quotes an ad in the *London Publick Adviser* of 1657 that lauds coffee as a "very wholesome and Physical drink" that apparently cured a variety of period ailments. The ad goes on to say that coffee "is good against Eye-sores, Coughs, or Colds, Rhumes, Consumption, Head-ach, Dropsie, Gout, Scurvy, and many others." Of course, Amsterdam physician Stefanus Blankaarts had his own comments: "[N]ext to the tea we have coffee, which is in use more in England than in Holland. It is, however, a drink not to be scorned and hardly less than tea, although she is not as agreeable of color, the taste is of roasted beans. She is healthful for those who like to drink her."

Customs and Paraphernalia

According to Amanda Lange, coffee cups are more U-shaped than teacups and usually have one, or possibly two, handles. Americans followed the English custom, and the first American coffeehouse was licensed in 1676 in Boston. Soon others appeared in New York and Philadelphia. In the mid- to late eighteenth century, Americans drank more and more coffee instead of tea to register their objection to the British tea taxes. Among the papers of Abraham de Peyster, I found a New York City merchant's account book listing a sale of half a pound each of coffee, tea and chocolate in the period from 1752 to 1756, indicating that all three beverages were enjoyed here. After 1776, coffee was imported from Haiti, Martinique and later Brazil. However, in the expression "a cup of Java," we still find a Dutch connection.

TEA

Common Stories of its Origins

It has long been assumed that tea drinking started in China about 2700 BC. It is not known exactly how—perhaps some leaves accidentally fell in boiling water and someone was attracted by the fragrance of the infusion. A Buddhist tale of the origin of tea relates the gruesome story of a monk cutting off his eyelids because he wanted to stay awake to meditate. In the place where he tossed the lids, tea bushes sprouted. Another tale relates that monks chewed tea leaves to combat sleepiness. Both stories point to tea's caffeine content. At first tea was used as a medicinal herb, which was seen to help clear the mind, as noted in a manuscript of around AD 300. By the sixth century, it had become an important trade article. While commonly associated with China and Japan, there is evidence of early use of tea in India as well. It is assumed that Buddhist monks spread the use of tea from China to Japan. It is also interesting to note that the way of making tea in these two countries is very different. In China, hot water is poured onto tea leaves, which is the method adopted by Europeans. In Japan, tea leaves were pulverized and then dissolved by whisking the powder in a small bowl with hot water, which gives the tea a somewhat porridge-like quality.

Varieties and Processing

Young shoots of tea are picked and brought in large baskets to the plantation's factory, where the leaves are spread in thin layers to allow moisture within the leaves to evaporate for twelve to eighteen hours. For black tea, the tea is then fermented by rolling the leaves between two turning surfaces, a process that frees the juices that give tea its specific taste. The still-moist leaves are then dried. For green tea, the fermentation step is omitted and the leaves are dried after the initial step.

Dutch Involvement in the Tea Trade

The earliest mention of tea in western literature dates to 1559. The earliest mention in Dutch comes from a travel journal several decades later, in which the Japanese tea ceremony is described. Contrary to what many think, it was the Dutch, not the English—now so closely associated with tea drinking—who brought the first shipment of tea to Europe in the year 1610. It was first considered a curiosity. In the early years of the tea trade, it was mostly Japanese tea, packed in narrow-necked jars, that was shipped to the Netherlands; but by the 1630s the tea trade increased, and tea from China, packed in tin-lined boxes, came to Holland through the intervention of Chinese traders in Batavia (now Jakarta) in Indonesia. Tea had become a popular daily drink in the Dutch East Indies in the first half of the seventeenth century, and apparently word of it reached the homeland. By 1667—when, for the first time, a large quantity of tea was brought to Amsterdam—there was a surprisingly large interest, and the tea trade started in earnest. Attempts were even made to grow tea in the Netherlands but without much success.

Period Comments

Stefanus Blankaarts said that tea is "the most healthful drink I have encountered so far, because the finest parts of the herb are steeped in hot water and are slurped by us, from twelve to twenty cups, it will thin our blood and juices [fluids]…it prevents all sorts of illnesses and is a cooling drink for fevers" (my translation).

A pamphlet from circa 1680, seemingly translated from Chinese, lists twenty-six virtues of tea drinking, among them that tea cleans the blood, chases away stupidity and sharpens the mind. In his treatise on "the most excellent herb tea" (1678), Cornelius Bontekoe of Dordrecht, another Dutch physician, has a similar but even stronger favorable opinion on the efficacy of the drink. In his work, he discusses the positive influence of tea on every part of the body. He even implied that drinking tea would give a person eternal life. Because of his propaganda, tea became generally well known in the Netherlands.

Through the above-mentioned works of Blankaarts and especially Bontekoe, tea drinking gained in popularity first for its medicinal and then for its pleasurable qualities. It became a drink for the intelligentsia and aristocracy and gradually found favor with the wealthy middle class. Bontekoe, so clearly in favor of tea drinking, was not happy that the lower classes would use it as a beverage, however, and as late as the end of the eighteenth century, a household manual suggested that maids should drink a glass of beer rather than a cup of tea so they would be nourished and work harder.

Customs and Paraphernalia

In the Netherlands, tea was drunk daily after the main meal, but the custom gradually moved to four or five o'clock. It became a social occasion for the women of the household, who would invite their friends to tea, to be enjoyed at a tea table set in the front of the house, later in the parlor or in a garden pavilion, which became known as a "tea pavilion." A logical byproduct of the tea trade was the tea paraphernalia, such as small pots for steeping, little teacups (smaller even than the ones we still see in Chinese restaurants), tea boxes and also lacquered and beautifully decorated tea tables. An early tea shipment of 1643 contained 1,400 pounds of tea and 7,675 pairs of teacups. (By the third decade of the century, Dutch potters tried to make their own version of porcelain, and from these attempts the now famous

Chinese teacup made for the European trade. *Photo by Richard Jacobs.*

blue and white Delftware resulted.) Later shipments contained as many as 500,000 pounds of tea but also other valuable products from China, such as silk, gold, lots of porcelain, lacquer work and even quicksilver. The woman of the house could spend a small fortune outfitting her parlor with fancy Oriental items.

Assembled around the tea table or other table with a tea tray, the custom was to try three or four different teas. The hostess would measure each tea in a small (red earthenware) pot and pour boiling water on the leaves. She would pour a little in each cup and add more water. The assembly would decide which tea was preferred and that was the one dispensed in larger quantities. There are stories of as many as twenty to fifty cups being consumed. I inherited a very old, small teacup such as those used then and measured how much liquid might have been consumed. It came to approximately five cups of liquid when downing twenty little cups. Needless to say, drinking that much fluid made it necessary to excuse oneself on occasion—that was done by saying one had to "mail a tea-letter."

Tea in New Netherland

Peter Kalm, assistant to Linnaeus, who came to America in 1749–50, described the eating habits of the Dutch in Albany. "Their breakfast is tea, commonly without milk...They never put sugar into the cup but take a small bit of it into their mouths while they drink." An account book of Joshua Delaplaine, a New York City merchant, lists a transaction in the period of 1752 to 1756 with his customer William Palmer, who bought sugar and tea and at one time even purchased three pounds of sugar and a half pound each of tea, coffee and chocolate. That tea drinking had become an important habit with the Dutch, English and anyone else in our valley and beyond we know from the "Boston Tea Party," caused by stringent English taxation and resulting in the subsequent War of Independence. We do have a Hudson Valley tea connection at Teatown Lake Reservation, a nature preserve and education center in Ossining. According to Lincoln Diamant in his book, *Images of America: Teatown Lake Reservation*, Revolutionary tradition has it that "a Manhattan greengrocer named John Arthur moved all his stock to this area in Westchester. Local gossip spread that his stock included tea" (for which he intended to get a fat profit). After a skirmish with the local women, he agreed to sell the tea at a fair price, hence the name Teatown.

SALT

Dutch Involvement in the Salt Trade

One of the pillars of Dutch wealth was the herring fisheries. A way of preserving was already found in the fourteenth century by partially gutting and salting the fish onboard ships. Clearly, if only for that industry, the Netherlands needed a large amount of salt. However, salt was also used for the preservation of all kinds of meat; in butter and cheese making; and in baking, salt controls yeast fermentation, to mention only a few of its many uses.

Since the early sixteenth century, salt was obtained outside the Netherlands, first from France and Germany and then from Spain and Portugal. Dutch ships dominated the salt trade with more than 60 percent of the trade and brought salt to the Baltic area. During the Eighty Years' War with Spain, King Philip II tried to force a Dutch surrender by cutting off the usual supplies from Setubal in Portugal. The result was not what he hoped for; his order simply forced the Dutch to go farther afield. First they went to the Cape Verde islands, where *zouthalers* (salt procurors) from the Dutch province of Zeeland had found salt. When large quantities of good salt were discovered along the north coast of Venezuela in Punta de Araya, dozens of Dutch ships were soon involved with obtaining salt there. It was a backbreaking job in the hot sun, but it was worth the effort. After the Spaniards had managed to build sturdy forts in the area during the twelve-year-long truce (1609–21), the Dutch moved on to salt pans on Curacao, Bonaire and St. Martin, which were conquered by the Dutch as a result.

Salt Processing

Salt is found in some places on earth close to the surface and can simply be dug up. Salt can also be obtained through the natural evaporation of seawater. The Netherlands does not have salt readily available, and the climate is not conducive to the evaporation method; therefore, another way of obtaining salt was devised. During medieval times, in the Dutch province of Zeeland, the salty peat bogs were dug, dried and then burned. The resulting *zel-as*, or salty ash, was mixed with seawater, and the salt was extracted by boiling down the mixture. In places such as Punta de Araya, reservoirs were dug along the coast, and thin layers of seawater were poured into these "salt pans." When the water evaporated, the salt was scraped into wheelbarrows and carted to the ships.

Period Comments

The Sensible Cook has an appendix called "The Dutch Butchering Time," with the subtitle "Instructing, how one shall supply oneself with a stock of Meat against the Winter." After instructions for preparing a wooden tub, it describes two ways of salting, the first method consisting of rubbing the meat with salt "all around on all sides and in all corners" and packing it into the tub as tightly as possible, with salt sprinkled between the layers. The second method used a brine in which to store the meat. The brine needs to be "so strong that no more salt will melt in it but an Egg will float in it."

Customs and Paraphernalia

To be seated "above the salt" has been an honor for centuries. To indicate such a place of honor, salt was served in beautifully decorated, elaborate silver saltcellars. The usual decorative salt stand was placed in the middle of the table, and the host was seated at the end. Those guests placed between the salt and the host—above the salt—were honored guests. Those seated toward the other end of the table—below the salt—were the less important persons. Seventeenth-century Dutch Masters such as Pieter Claes or Floris van Dijck portray the saltcellars in their still lifes.

Salt in New Netherland

Elaborate Dutch silver saltcellars are part of the collections of museums in the Hudson Valley, including the Metropolitan Museum in New York City. The Albany Institute of History and Art owns a standing salt topped with three small tulip buds, attributed to Gaef Mendertsz and made in the city of Haarlem in 1652. The saltcellar was for many years in the possession of the Hun family. It is an example of a number of pieces made in the Netherlands that have passed along from generation to generation in New York families. Silver in the colony, as well as in the homeland, was an important social symbol, demonstrating not only the wealth acquired but also the close acquaintance with superior culture and the latest fashions of the mother country.

SPICES

Common Stories of their Origins

To discuss the origin of each spice would not fit into this thumbnail sketch format.

Pepper, ginger and cardamom have been known since antiquity, followed later by cinnamon, nutmeg, mace, cloves and galingale, transported overland from Asia to the Levant and from there to Venice and beyond. We might add saffron to that list as a most expensive trade item. Professor Van Winter says that "in the Middle Ages it became obligatory in haute cuisine." Apparently it was not used for its taste but for its coloring.

Spice Processing

Spices were shipped whole in dried form; because they were light, easy to transport and profitable, they were a favored trade item. Spices such as cinnamon, cloves, nutmeg or mace were used whole or pounded in a mortar with a pestle. *De Verstandige Kock* (*The Sensible Cook*) contains recipes calling for whole nutmeg, or nutmeg cut into four or six parts, to be cooked in stews of multiple meats and vegetables.

Dutch Involvement in the Spice Trade

The Dutch were not the first in the spice trade by any means. Spices were first traded through Venice, and subsequently

Portuguese traders became involved. By the 1590s, the first Dutch expeditions started toward the East Indies. According to Julie Berger-Hochstrasser in her book on trade items that appear in Dutch still lifes, the second East India expedition brought some 600,000 pounds of pepper and altogether 250,000 pounds of cloves, nutmeg and mace, which netted investors a 400 percent profit. The Dutch East India Company was founded in 1602 and became heavily involved in the spice trade.

Period Comments

Stefanus Blankaarts enumerated the following herbs and spices: pepper, cinnamon, nutmeg, cloves, oregano, ginger, saffron, turmeric, onions, garlic, mustard seed, coriander, anise and chervil. He was particularly enamored of the use of cloves. "One should use this as much as possible," he admonished, but he found all of them quite healthful.

Customs and Paraphernalia

In one of his still lifes, Willem Kalf portrayed a nutmeg grater that looked like its modern counterpart. Another very handy device for grating various foodstuffs is the rasp (now making a comeback). Various paintings by Dutch Masters showed rasps hanging on the wall. Spices were expensive and were often kept in boxes under lock and key in the homeland, as well as in New Netherland.

Spices in New Netherland

Russell Shorto mentioned that when Adriaen van der Donck came back to New Netherland after a long sojourn in the homeland, he brought with him a hundred pounds of pepper, no doubt to be used for trading. Quantities of spices are listed on the cargo lists of New Netherland traders such as Frederick and Adolph Philipse. For our exhibit, Matters of Taste, at the

Albany Institute of History and Art in 2002, we received a loan of a spice cabinet belonging to a descendant of Anneke Jans, a seventeenth-century (female) Dutch settler of Albany.

SUGAR

Common Stories of its Origin

Sugar's origin lies in the Ganges region of India. There is mention of it as far back as 1200 BC. Its use gradually spread throughout the Middle East. By the end of the first millennium, Venice was trading sugar with central Europe. Around the same time, Arabs installed a sugar refinery on Crete; Muslims grew sugar on the Greek islands, as well as on Sicily; and the Crusaders became acquainted with sugar on their trips to the Holy Land. As early as 1506, the Spanish began cultivating sugar on Cuba and Hispaniola, and the Portuguese started large plantations in Brazil.

During the seventeenth century, the Dutch conquered Recife in Brazil, and New Holland was established there by 1636, governed by Johan Maurits, Count of Nassau Siegen, a tolerant man. Because of his tolerance, Jews and other groups persecuted by the fanatically Catholic Spanish moved to New Holland. The Dutch took over the sugar plantations of the Portuguese in Brazil but continued to depend on their production knowledge.

Sugar Processing

Sugar cane was cut and brought to a central place for processing. There it was milled to extract the juice, which was then boiled and carefully skimmed. The purified juice was concentrated to syrup by evaporation. Further evaporation crystallizes the syrup with the byproduct of (liquid) molasses. Another product from sugar processing is rum, made from fermented sugar cane juice. At the end of processing, the partially refined brown sugar was shipped to the Netherlands, where it was refined further. By the 1640s, Amsterdam had several dozen refineries. The final product was sold as white sugar cones by the "sugar baker."

Dutch Involvement in the Sugar Trade

Sugar production was backbreaking work and became entirely dependent on slave labor, as the indigenous population could not survive it. Through the sugar trade in Brazil, the Dutch became involved in the slave trade, and by 1644, they delivered as many as five thousand slaves to New Holland. By the 1660s, Curacao was the biggest slave depot in the Caribbean. By the end of the century, the Dutch slave trade intensified, and they even monopolized the *asiento* trade (delivery of slaves to the Spanish territories).

Period Comments

Stefanus Blankaarts admonished, "All sugar and confitures, when eaten too much, have no usefulness for our body." He continued by remarking that white sugar is better because the lye used in the refining process would take away extra acid from the body. He asserted that most (period) physicians agreed on the harmfulness of sugar and therefore did not prescribe it anymore. (This was still a time when sugar was considered a medicine.)

Customs and Paraphernalia

Sugar cones were cut into pieces with the aid of a large metal cutter, or "nipper." The pieces of sugar were then pounded in a mortar with a pestle for use in recipes. It was not until the middle of the nineteenth century that milled granulated sugar became available. Before sugar was used as the sweetener that we know nowadays, it was used in medicine. You might remember the line in the song from *Mary Poppins*—"a spoonful of sugar makes the medicine go down." It was used to preserve fruits, but often the fruits were then used for medicinal purposes, as for instance in a recipe in *The Sensible Confectioner* (another appendix to *The Sensible Cook*), where it was used for a syrup of currants, which was recommended "for hot fevers." The anonymous author went on the say, "There has not been found a better cooling than this for the Tongue." Sugar was also used as a coating for seeds or nuts. Today we still know sugarcoated almonds or "Jordan almonds," often given in small goodie bags at weddings. In the Netherlands, births were celebrated with a special drink called *kandeel*, which was accompanied by sugared thin cinnamon sticks or seeds, treats called *kapittelstokken*. Continuing that tradition to the present time, whenever a child is born, rusks with butter and sugarcoated anise seeds are dispensed as a treat.

Sugar in New Netherland

While there is no record of sugarcoated nuts or seeds in New Netherland, fruits were certainly preserved by boiling with sugar, and we do have recipes in the cookbooks belonging to descendants of the early Dutch settlers for such preservation methods. In those books, recipes for "condale," the anglicized name for *kandeel*, the drink served at births, can also be found. This demonstrates once again that recipes are not only instructions on how to cook, but also serve as indications of social customs.

Chapter 10

THE PROOF IS IN THE PUDDING

T he proof is indeed in the pudding when we taste historical
recipes. They tell us about the kinds of food that were
eaten and the flavors that were enjoyed. With the following
recipes you can make a delicious modern menu for entertaining
and at the same time give your guests an enticing taste of the
Hudson Valley's past. The artichoke salad or the asparagus on
toast will make fine first courses. The meatballs with orange
can be served with the parsnips and the peas and, to keep the
menu in seventeenth-century style, accompanied by the *duivekater*
bread (remember that no potatoes were eaten at the time). Apple
custard will make a delightful ending to the meal. Beverages
might be ginger beer, beer or wine. Other little menus can be
made, as well, such as a cup of frothy cocoa with some New
Year's cakes as a winter afternoon treat. The Dutch pancakes
accompanied by applesauce or hot, moist Seneca cornbread,
slathered with butter and paired with thick-sliced bacon, can be
proudly presented as a hearty breakfast.

RECIPES

From Chapter 1

The first recipe comes from my translation of the 1683 edition of *De Verstandige Kock* (*The Sensible Cook*). The combination of artichokes and radishes, both spring vegetables, is not only very pretty, but it is tasty as well.

Artichoke Salad with Radishes

1 artichoke per person (if very large, use half)
Bacon
Beef broth
Radishes
Cress

Dressing:
Oil, wine vinegar, salt, pepper, dash of sugar and minced green herbs.

Wrap each artichoke in bacon slices and cook in the beef broth until done (the bottom can be pierced with a fork). Cool in the broth. When cool, remove the leaves, discard the fuzzy choke and thin leaves and cut the bottom into eight parts. Arrange them on a plate and surround them with some of the leaves (cut off sharp tips). Decorate with the washed radishes, either whole or cut in half, and place one radish in the middle, perhaps on a little bed of cress if available. Combine the dressing ingredients; sprinkle the salad lightly with the dressing and serve.

From Chapter 2

Four meatball recipes appear in the 1683 edition of *The Sensible Cook*, the definitive Dutch cookbook of the seventeenth century. All four are made with veal, and the first one seasons the meatballs with grated lemon or orange zest. The recipe says that "it gives a very good smell and flavor," and the anonymous author is right that it does! In the second recipe, the meatballs are first boiled and then fried in butter. The third recipe wraps the meat around a (hard-boiled) egg and places the combination inside a small head of lettuce. These are also boiled, and the broth is thickened with crushed rusk and flavored with butter and *verjuice* (juice of unripe grapes). In the last recipe, the flavored meat is wrapped in bacon slices sprinkled with chopped parsley—it is a forerunner of a modern Dutch dish often referred to as *slavinken*, which essentially follows the same process minus the parsley. All four recipes are delicious, but my favorite is the first one. Apparently it was a favorite with New Netherland settlers as well; the same recipe can also be found in the handwritten cookbooks of descendants of those early settlers. For instance, it appears in the book written by Anne Stevenson van Cortlandt (1784–1821).

Veal Meatballs with Orange

1 pound ground veal
2 slices whole grain bread, soaked in milk and squeezed dry
1 egg
1 tablespoon minced onion
1 tablespoon minced celery
Pinch dried thyme
Pinch ground cloves
Pinch ground allspice
Grated zest of 1 orange
1 teaspoon salt
Freshly ground pepper

Dash of cayenne pepper
Oil or butter for frying

In a large bowl, thoroughly combine all ingredients (except oil or butter) and shape into four to six balls. Heat oil or butter in a frying pan and brown the meatballs on all sides. Add $1/3$ cup of water or broth, cover the pan and simmer until done, about twenty minutes, depending on size. These can also be made in a small size ($1\frac{1}{2}$ inch) and used as hot hors d'oeuvres.

From Chapter 3

The reason that I included an apple custard to represent the bread chapter is that in this recipe bread is used as a thickener, which was a very common use. It is another adaptation from *The Sensible Cook*. Its consistency is reminiscent of tapioca pudding, but if you prefer a smoother texture, you can mash the bread very fine and make sure the custard is smooth. This recipe captures the essence of apple with its bright, mouth-filling flavor and makes the perfect fall dessert; nowadays, however, it can be enjoyed anytime.

Apple Custard

2¼ pounds Golden Delicious apples
½ cup dry white wine
½ cup water
2 tablespoons butter
1 cup coarse fresh bread crumbs without crust, made from a good peasant-style white bread
5 egg yolks
½ teaspoon ground ginger
2–4 tablespoons sugar to taste

Peel the apples, quarter and core. Cut each quarter in three slices lengthwise and then cut the slices across into small pieces. In a large saucepan, combine the wine, water, butter and apple pieces. Cook until the apples are very soft. Mash the apples and stir in the bread crumbs and then mash the crumbs as well. Whisk in the egg yolks, ginger and sugar and cook over low heat, stirring constantly about three to four minutes, until the custard thickens. Pour into a pretty bowl and serve at room temperature or chilled. The custard is delicious by itself, but if you like you could accompany it with some plain butter cookies.

From Chapter 4

The next recipe is for the Seneca corn bread taught to me by George Heron. It is completely different from today's much drier baked corn bread. Plimoth Plantation in Plymouth, Massachusetts, which tells the story of the Pilgrims and the local Wampanoag people, uses similar corn and similar methods to prepare bread at the Wampanoag homesite.

Seneca Boiled Corn Bread

3 cups white cornmeal
1 (15-ounce) can pinto beans, drained and rinsed
1½ cups boiling water

Before you start making the bread, place a kettle on the stove and fill it three quarters full with water and bring it to a boil.

In a shallow bowl place the cornmeal and mix with the pinto beans. Push to the side of the bowl and pour in about a cup of the boiling water. Stir and combine.

Every recipe for this bread says, as George Heron did, "Too much water—dough gets mushy; too little water—dough gets dry," so add the rest of the boiling water a little at a time as needed to make a dough that hangs together well. Rinse your hands, and with wet hands take up a portion of dough, make a ball and flatten it into a five-inch wheel about two inches thick. Smooth any crack with a little water. Keep your hands wet so the dough does not stick. Use a wide spatula and carefully slide the wheel into the kettle with the boiling water. Stand it on end at an angle against the side of the kettle and proceed in the same way with the other wheels. Boil for twenty minutes. They will float to the top when done. If necessary, loosen them from the side of the kettle. Set out pieces of aluminum foil and place a wheel on each. Allow steam to come out a bit and then wrap. They'll continue to cook, and according to George Heron, "They will be moist that way." Serve hot or cooled.

From Chapter 5

The recipes from the books in the archives of the Huguenot Historical Society in New Paltz, New York, give a unique insight into the cultural changes that took place in a rural area of New York State. They cover a period of about 140 years from the beginning of the nineteenth century through 1940. They demonstrate how descendants of the original French Huguenot patentees and others with whom they intermarried changed and became increasingly more American, as evidenced for instance by recipes for Washington Cake or Lincoln Cake, while other recipes illustrate a continuing connection with the French homeland or show the Dutch influence. From these books I chose (and adapted) three vegetable recipes and a pancake recipe to represent these connections.

Asparagus on Toast

1 pound asparagus with thin stalks
Salt
¼ teaspoon sugar
4 long chives
4 slices whole wheat or white bread for toast
Butter
Optional: freshly grated nutmeg

Break off the hard ends of the asparagus and wash them. Place them in a saucepan large enough to hold them in one layer and pour on enough water to almost cover them. Add salt to taste and the sugar. Bring to a boil and cook for two or three minutes until barely done. Take them out of the water with a spatula (save the water). Cool somewhat and divide the asparagus into bunches and tie with a chive into a little bundle. In the meantime, toast the bread and butter it. Place the asparagus bundles on the toast. Pour off all but ¼ cup of the cooking water and add two tablespoons of butter. Stir to melt the butter. Drizzle just a little of the cooking water over the bundles and grate on some nutmeg if you like that combination. Serve at once. This makes a lovely first course any time thin asparagus are available.

The following deceptively simple recipe can be made very successfully using frozen "petite peas" to create an unusual and succulent dish. The sugar and egg yolk accent and heighten the pea flavor.

Peas with Sugar

$\frac{1}{2}$ cup boiling water
2 teaspoons sugar
$\frac{1}{2}$ teaspoon salt
1 (10-ounce) package frozen petite peas
1 tablespoon butter
1 egg yolk

In a small saucepan, combine water, sugar and salt and bring to a boil. Add the peas and cook for three minutes while stirring to separate the peas. Drain most of the water and stir in the butter and egg yolk. Reduce heat and cook two minutes over low heat, while stirring until yolk is incorporated and cooked. Serve at once as a side dish to the meatballs, pork or ham.

Sautéed Parsnips

1 pound parsnips, washed and cleaned
Salt
4 tablespoons butter
Finely chopped parsley

Scrape the parsnips and cut into two-inch sticks. Boil in water with salt until barely done. Drain. Heat the butter in a frying pan and sauté the sticks until lightly browned. Sprinkle with parsley and serve as a side dish to the meatballs, turkey cutlets or ham.

Recipes for pancakes, similar to the one that follows, appear in *The Sensible Cook* as well.

Pancakes in the Dutch Manner

3 large eggs
Water
2 cups flour
¼ teaspoon (scant) ground nutmeg
¼ teaspoon (scant) mace
¼ teaspoon (scant) cloves
Pinch of salt
Butter

Beat the eggs with a few tablespoons of water until light. Measure the liquid; you should have at least 1½ cups, if not, add more water. In a medium bowl, combine flour, spices and salt. Stir in the liquid to make a smooth batter. Heat two tablespoons butter in a frying pan or pancake pan with sloping sides. To make a five-inch pancake, use ⅓ cup batter; if necessary, level the top with a spoon to make the pancake about ¼-inch thick. Fry on both sides until brown. Repeat with the rest of the batter. Top each pancake with a pat of butter and sprinkle with sugar. Some (homemade) applesauce is a nice accompaniment. The recipe makes four to five pancakes.

From Chapter 6

In her essay on spices and comfits, Johanna Maria van Winter discusses "look-alikes, imitation foods that recalled the memory [of] the eggs and flesh the Church denied [during periods of fasting]." She mentions the holiday bread, for which the recipe follows, and thinks that it goes back much farther than the seventeenth century. It is a dough made to resemble an ox shank (though it is made in other forms as well, as we can see in the Dusart drawing in Chapter 6). The ox shank shape was to recreate an animal or animal part during the time of fasting, when the Catholic Church forbade the consumption of four-footed animal products. The name *duivekater* is somewhat of a mystery but is believed to be a contraction of the Dutch words *duivel* (devil) and *kater* (tomcat). Why? No one has figured that out as yet. It is a lovely buttery bread that keeps quite well and is delicious toasted with butter and topped with (homemade) jam.

Duivekater (Buttery, Lemon-flavored Holiday Bread)

¼ cup warm water (100–110 degrees)
2 packages active dry yeast
Pinch of sugar
4 cups all-purpose or bread flour
¼ teaspoon salt
Zest of 1 lemon
1 egg yolk
¾ cup lukewarm milk
½ cup sugar
1 stick butter, melted and cooled
1 egg, beaten with a fork

Pour the warm water into a small bowl and sprinkle with the yeast and the sugar. Let stand for a moment and then stir to dissolve the yeast. Set aside in a warm place. Scoop the flour into the bowl of an electric mixer, equipped with a dough hook; add the salt and zest and gently stir to combine. Add the egg yolk to the milk and beat to combine. Pour into the flour mixture; add the sugar, stir to combine on a low setting. Then pour in the butter and yeast and beat for five minutes, again on a low setting. The dough will be smooth and soft. Very lightly flour a counter and knead the dough by hand for five more minutes, slapping it hard on the counter a few times. Butter a large bowl; form the dough into a ball and place it in the greased bowl, rotating the dough to grease the entire surface. Let the dough rise, covered, in a warm place for about one and a half hours or until doubled in bulk. Punch down the dough, remove from the bowl and shape it into a loaf that is pointed on each end. Place on a baking sheet and let the loaf rise for about thirty to forty-five minutes.

Preheat the oven to 350 degrees.

To form the *duivekater*, you have two choices. You can make it to resemble the bread in the Dusart drawing in Chapter 6 and form a diamond and decorate the top of the dough with a pattern of razor gashes. Or you can create a bread to resemble an ox shank as follows. Cut into one end three times; the other end twice. Form those cut pieces into loose curl shapes. With scissors, cut into both sides of the loaf from end to end. Using a razor blade cut a pleasing pattern in the middle of the dough. For either shape (diamond or ox shank), carefully brush the loaf with beaten egg. Do not brush into the gashes, so you get a two-toned loaf. Bake in the preheated oven for about forty-five to fifty-five minutes or until nicely browned and an instant thermometer, carefully inserted in the side of the bread, reads 220 degrees Fahrenheit. Remove and cool on a rack.

From Chapter 7

In the winter of 1989–90, a curator discovered "Mrs. Lefferts' book" (the handwritten cookbook belonging to Maria Lott Lefferts, 1786–1865) in the attic of the Lefferts house, now part of Prospect Park in Brooklyn. It contains a recipe for New Year's cakes. Over the course of the years, I have made several modern-day adaptations. The recipe that follows I like the best because it is a much simpler and much smaller version of hers, which calls for "28 lb of flour 10 lb of Sugar 5lb of Butter carraway seed and Orange peal" and is again proof that a large amount of cookies was needed to distribute to the hundreds of visitors on New Year's Day. The addition of grated orange zest makes a tangy, perfect flavor combination with the customary caraway seeds.

Mrs. Lefferts' New Year's Cakes (Thin Caraway- and Orange-flavored Cookies)

4 cups all-purpose flour, sifted
1 cup light brown sugar, packed
½ teaspoon salt
8 tablespoons (1 stick) butter
1 egg, lightly beaten
½ cup milk, plus more if needed
1 tablespoon caraway seed, crushed somewhat with a
  rolling pin to release flavor
Grated zest of 1 orange

Sift all dry ingredients into a large bowl. If sifting the sugar is problematic, rub it between your hands to make sure no lumps remain. Use a dough blender or two knives to cut in the butter until the mixture looks like coarse meal. In a small bowl or measuring cup, beat the egg and milk, pour into the flour/butter mixture and add the seeds and zest. If the dough seems too stiff, add a little more milk a tablespoon at a time. Knead the dough until it comes together; wrap and cool for one hour or overnight.

Preheat the oven to 300 degrees. Lightly flour a counter or board. Divide the dough into three parts (it is easier to roll out in small portions, one at a time) and roll each part as thin as possible. Cut out with small cookies cutters or cut the rolled dough into small diamond shapes. Transfer to buttered baking sheet and bake until pale brown and crisp, about thirty minutes. Yield: at least six dozen, depending on size.

From Chapter 8
Years ago, Mary Young and Evelyne Richardson of Harlem, New York, who prepared African food at one of the early Pinkster Festivals held at Philipsburg Manor in Sleepy Hollow, New York, gave me the following recipe for a wonderful, seemingly intoxicating, yet nonalcoholic drink.

Ginger Beer

1 cup minced fresh ginger (about $\frac{1}{2}$ pound)
1 quart boiling water
Juice of 2 lemons
$3\frac{1}{2}$ cups pineapple juice
Generous dash of freshly grated nutmeg
Sugar to taste

In a quart jar combine ginger and water and steep for three hours. Strain liquid into a large pitcher; add the lemon and pineapple juices. Stir in the nutmeg. Taste and add sugar as necessary. Serve over ice cubes.

The ginger beer is also very good as a cocktail. For every 8 ounces of ginger beer add $1\frac{1}{2}$ ounces of light rum. A great drink for a hot summer's day!

From Chapter 9

The following recipe is the result of my research on chocolate. After learning about the centuries-old ways of making hot chocolate, flavored with spices, I created my own recipe using unsweetened baking chocolate, spices and sugar. Serve the drink in four-ounce cups. It has a large amount of caffeine, so taste it before you consider serving it to children and, if you are prone to sleepless nights, drink it in the morning rather than the evening.

Hot Chocolate, the Old/New Way

4 squares unsweetened baking chocolate, cut into
   quarters
$\frac{1}{2}$ teaspoon cinnamon
$\frac{1}{8}$ teaspoon cayenne pepper, or more
$\frac{1}{4}$ teaspoon ground ginger
3–4 teaspoons sugar, or to your taste
2 cups boiling water and 2 cups boiling whole milk
OR 2 cups boiling water and 2 cups boiling half and half
$\frac{1}{2}$ teaspoon vanilla extract

Process the chocolate pieces in a food processor outfitted with a metal blade until they are reduced to fine granules. Place the chocolate in a saucepan, large enough to hold a quart of liquid. Add the cinnamon, cayenne, ginger and sugar. Pour on the boiling water slowly and stir with a whisk to dissolve the chocolate; add the vanilla and milk or half and half. Whisk over low heat until incorporated; keep on whisking to create a frothy drink. Makes eight four-ounce cups. Note: some household stores (e.g. Williams-Sonoma) now sell chocolate pots with a battery-operated "frother."

NOTES AND LIST OF BOOKS CONSULTED

In the text, many sources are mentioned in their entirety, here are only those that need further elaboration. They are listed in the order that they appear in the various chapters.

CHAPTER 1: HISTORICAL OVERVIEW

Israel, Jonathan I. *The Dutch Republic: Its Rise, Greatness and Fall, 1477–1806.* Oxford History of Early Europe. Oxford: Clarendon Press, 1998.

New Netherland Institute. www.nnp.org.

Schaefer, Vincent J. *Dutch Barns of New York: An Introduction.* Fleischmanns, NY: Purple Mountain Press, 1994.

Blackburn, Roderic H., et al. *Dutch Colonial Homes in America.* New York: Rizzoli, 2002.

Blackburn, Roderic H., and Ruth Piwonka. *Remembrance of Patria: Dutch Arts and Culture in Colonial America, 1609–1776.* Albany, NY: Albany Institute of History and Art, 1988.

Dilliard, Maud Esther. *An Album of New Netherland.* New York: Bramhall House, 1963.

CHAPTER 2: THE INFLUENCE OF THE DUTCH ON THE AMERICAN KITCHEN

Burema, Lambertus. *De Voeding in Nederland van de Middeleeuwen tot de Twintigste Eeuw.* Assen, Drenthe: Van Gorcum, 1953.

Rose, Peter G., trans. and ed. *The Sensible Cook: Dutch Foodways in the Old and the New World.* Syracuse, NY: Syracuse University Press, 1998.

Van Winter, Johanna Maria. *Spices and Comfits: Collected Papers on Medieval Food.* Devon, UK: Prospect Books, 2007.

Van der Donck, Adriaen. *A Description of the New Netherlands.* Edited with an introduction by Thomas F. O'Donnel. Syracuse, NY: Syracuse University Press, 1968.

————. *A Description of New Netherland.* Edited by Charles T. Gehring and William A. Starna and translated by Diederik Willem Goedhuys, with a foreword by Russell Shorto. Lincoln: University of Nebraska Press, 2008.

Kalm, Peter. *Travels in North America: The English Version of 1770.* Edited by Adolph B. Benson. Two vols. Mineola, NY: Dover, 1966.

Grant, Anne. *Memoirs of an American Lady.* 1901. Reprint. Freeport, NY: Books for Libraries Press, 1972.

CHAPTER 3: BEER AND BREAD

Schama, Simon. *The Embarassment of Riches: An Interpretation of Dutch Culture in the Golden Age.* New York: Alfred A. Knopf, 1987.

Scott, Kenneth. *New Amsterdam's Taverns and Tavernkeepers,* I, II, III, IV and V in *De Halve Maen: Journal of the Holland Society of New York* (April 1964–April 1965).

Folkerts, Jan. "Kiliaen Van Rensselaer and the Agricultural Productivity in His Domain: A New Look at the First Patroon and Rensselaerswijck before 1664." Paper delivered at Rensselaerswijck Seminar, Albany, NY, 1986.

————. "Farming for Bread and Beer: the commercial nature of New Netherland agriculture and the staffs of life." Paper delivered at Rensselaerswijck Seminar, Albany, NY, 1996.

Kistemaker, Renee and Carry Lakerveld, eds. *Brood, Aardappels en Patat: eeuwen eten in Amsterdam*. Amsterdam, Netherlands: Amsterdam Historisch Museum, 1983.

McGants, Anne. "Monotonous but not Meager: the Diet of Burgher Orphans in Early Modern Amsterdam." Research in *Economic History* 14 (1992): 69–116.

Van Deursen, A. Th. *Het Kopergeld van de Gouden Eeuw: het Dagelijks Brood*. Assen, Drenthe: Van Gorcum, 1981.

Venema, Janny, trans. and ed. *Deacons' Accounts, 1652–1674 Beverwijck/Albany*. The Historical Series of the Reformed Church in America, No. 28. Rockland, ME: Picton Press, 1998.

CHAPTER 4: BREAD AND *SAPAEN*: FOOD WAYS OF THE DUTCH AND IROQUOIS

Dunn, Shirley. *The Mohicans and Their Land 1609–1730*. Fleischmanns, NY: Purple Mountain Press, 1994.

Gehring, Charles T., and William A. Starna, trans. and eds. *A Journey into Mohawk and Oneida Country, 1634–1635*. Syracuse, NY: Syracuse University Press, 1988.

Seaver, James. *The Life of Mary Jemison*. 1982 edition. Published by the American Scenic and Historic Preservation Society.

Parker, Arthur C. *Parker on the Iroquois: Iroquois Uses of Maize and Other Food Plants; The Code of Handsome Lake, the Seneca Prophet; The Constitution of the Five Nations*. Edited with an introduction by William N. Fenton. Syracuse, NY: Syracuse University Press, 1968.

Kalm, Peter. *Travels in North America: The English Version of 1770*. Edited by Adolph B. Benson. Two vols. Mineola, NY: Dover, 1966.

CHAPTER 5: TASTE OF CHANGE

Irving, Washington. *A History of New York, by Diedrich Knickerbocker.* Edited by Edwin T. Bowden. New York: Twayne Publishers, 1964.

Grant, Anne. *Memoirs of an American Lady.* 1901. Reprint. Freeport, NY: Books for Libraries Press, 1972.

Randolph, Mary. *The Virginia Housewife.* Facsimile edited by Karen Hess. Columbia: University of South Carolina Press, 1984.

CHAPTER 6: THE SAINT NICHOLAS CELEBRATION

Seal, Jeremy: *Nicholas: The Epic Journey from Saint to Santa Claus.* London: Bloomsbury Publishing, 2005.

Jones, Charles W. *Saint Nicholas of Myra, Bari, and Manhattan: Biography of a Legend.* Chicago: The University of Chicago Press, 1988. [This must be the most definitive book on Saint Nicholas, and the main historical information in this chapter is based on it.]

Shorto, Russell. *The Island at the Center of the World: The Epic Story of Dutch Manhattan & the Forgotten Colony that Shaped America.* New York: Doubleday, 2004.

CHAPTER 7: THE DUTCH NEW YEAR'S CELEBRATION

Lyman, Susan E. "New Year's Day in 1861." *New York Historical Society Quarterly* 26 (January 1944).

Chesterfield, Philip Dormer Stanhope. Chesterfield's Art of Letter-Writing Simplified...to which is Appended the Complete Rules of Etiquette, and the Usages of Society. N.p.: 1860.

Hamlin, Huybertie Pruyn. *An Albany Girlhood.* Edited by Alice P. Kenney. Washington, D.C.: Washington Park Press Ltd., 1990.

The Rapalje Cotheal Collection, vols. 22–44, in the archives of the Fishkill Historical Society.

CHAPTER 8: THE PINXTER CELEBRATION

Danckaerts, Jasper. *Journal of Jasper Danckaerts, 1679–1680.* Edited by Barlett Burleigh James and J. Franklin Jameson. New York: Charles Scribner's Sons, 1913.

Background information in this chapter is based on the research for a paper for the interpretive staff, kindly shared with me by Jackie Haley of Historic Hudson Valley in 1984 and on an article given to me by David Steven Cohen, at the time coordinator of the Folklife Program for the New Jersey Historical Commission, entitled "In Search of Carolus Africanus Rex: Afro-Dutch Folklore in New York and New Jersey."

Williams-Myers, A.J. "Pinkster Carnival: Africanisms in the Hudson Valley" in *Afro-Americans in New York Life and History* (January 1985).

CHAPTER 9: CACAO, COFFEE AND TEA; SALT, SPICES AND SUGAR

Coe, Sophie D., and Michael D. Coe. *The True History of Chocolate.* New York: Thames & Hudson, 1993.

Young, Allen M. *The Chocolate Tree: A Natural History of Cacao.* Revised and expanded edition. Gainesville: University Press of Florida, 2007.

Berry, Sara S. *Fathers Work for their Sons: Accumulation, Mobility and Class Formation in an Extended Yoruba Community.* Berkeley: University of California Press, 1985.

Satre, Lowell J. *Chocolate on Trial: Slavery, Politics & the Ethics of Business.* Athens: Ohio University Press, 2005.

Klooster, Wim. *Illicit Riches: Dutch Trade in the Caribbean, 1648–1795*. Koninklijk Instituut voor Taal, Land-en Volkenkunde, Caribbean Series, 18. Leiden, Netherlands: KITLV Press, 1998. [This is a must-read for anyone interested in the Dutch Caribbean trade.]

Tannahill, Reay. *Food in History*. New, fully revised and updated edition. New York: Crown Publishers, Inc., 1988.

Bates, Robert H. *Open-Economy Politics: The Political Economy of the World Coffee Trade*. Princeton, NJ: Princeton University Press, 1997.

Museum Boymans-van Beuningen. *Thema Thee: de geschiedenis van de thee en het theegebruik in Nederland*. Rotterdam, Netherlands: Museum Boymans-van Beuningen, 1978.

Account book of Joshua Delaplaine in the archives of the New York Historical Society.

Museum Boymans-van Beuningen. *Zout of Tafel: de geschiedenis van het zoutvat*. Rotterdam, Netherlands: Museum Boymans-van Beuningen, 1976.

Spruit, Ruud. *Zout en Slaven: De geschiedenis van de Westindische Compagnie*. Houten, Netherlands: De Haan/Unieboek bv, 1988.

Krondl, Michael. *The Taste of Conquest: The Rise and Fall of the Three Great Cities of Spice*. New York: Ballantine Books, 2007.

Turner, Jack. *Spice: the History of a Temptation*. New York: Alfred A. Knopf, 2004.

Berger-Hochstrasser, Julie. *Still Life and Trade in the Dutch Golden Age*. New Haven, CT: Yale University Press, 2007.

Mintz, Sidney W. *Sweetness and Power: The Place of Sugar in Modern History*. New York: Penguin Books, 1985.

INDEX

ABOUT THE AUTHOR

 Peter G. Rose is a woman. She was born in the Netherlands and came to the United States in the mid-1960s. She has worked as a food writer and contributed a syndicated column on family food and cooking to the New York–based Gannett newspapers for more than twenty years. She has written articles for magazines such as *Gourmet* and *Saveur*, as well as for newspapers and magazines in the Netherlands and locally for *Hudson Valley Magazine* and the *Valley Table*.

She started her research on the influence of the Dutch on the American kitchen in the early 1980s and published her first book on the subject, *The Sensible Cook: Dutch Foodways in the Old and the New World*, at the end of that decade. It was followed by *Foods of the Hudson: A Seasonal Sampling of the Region's Bounty* (1993) and *Matters of Taste: Food and Drink in Seventeenth-Century Dutch Art and Life* (2002) with Dr. Donna R. Barnes.

As a member of the Speakers in the Humanities program of the New York Council for the Humanities, she lectures on historic Dutch food ways all over New York State. She illustrates her talks with paintings of the Dutch Masters and has spoken at many museums with holdings of such Dutch art all around America. She lives with her husband, Don, in South Salem, New York, in the beautiful, historic Hudson Valley. Please visit her website: www.peterrose.com.

Visit us at
www.historypress.net